Skill Versus Luck

Skill Versus Luck

Taking the Guessing Out of Equity Fund Selection

Michael A. Ervolini

The MIT Press
Cambridge, Massachusetts
London, England

The MIT Press
Massachusetts Institute of Technology
77 Massachusetts Avenue
Cambridge, MA 02139
mitpress.mit.edu

The MIT Press would like to thank the anonymous peer reviewers who provided comments on drafts of this book. The generous work of academic experts is essential for establishing the authority and quality of our publications. We acknowledge with gratitude the contributions of these otherwise uncredited readers.

This book was set in Stone Serif and Stone Sans by Westchester Publishing Services. Printed and bound in the United States of America.

Library of Congress Cataloging-in-Publication Data

Names: Ervolini, Michael A., 1955– author
Title: Skill versus luck : taking the guessing out of equity fund selection / Michael A. Ervolini.
Description: Cambridge, Massachusetts : The MIT Press, [2026] | Includes bibliographical references.
Identifiers: LCCN 2025019750 (print) | LCCN 2025019751 (ebook) | ISBN 9780262052184 hardcover | ISBN 9780262052191 pdf | ISBN 9780262052207 epub
Subjects: LCSH: Portfolio management | Investment analysis
Classification: LCC HG4529.5 .E783 2026 (print) | LCC HG4529.5 (ebook) | DDC 332.63/22—dc23/eng/20250904
LC record available at https://lccn.loc.gov/2025019750
LC ebook record available at https://lccn.loc.gov/2025019751

10 9 8 7 6 5 4 3 2 1

EU Authorised Representative: Easy Access System Europe, Mustamäe tee 50, 10621 Tallinn, Estonia | Email: gpsr.requests@easproject.com

To my wife, Jeanne, for all you do to make my life so incredible

Contents

Contents

Foreword

It is a distinct pleasure writing the foreword for this book. One reason is that in it Mike is addressing a critical issue impacting equity management (and active management generally): How can we do a better job at assessing manager skill? Another reason is that, after decades with one of the world's largest sovereign wealth funds working with internal and external management teams, I know firsthand how difficult it is to separate skill from luck when assessing fund results. Lastly, I have gotten to know Mike pretty well over the past several years and think his views on fund management, and particularly those regarding institutional capital allocations, are thought-provoking and well worth reading. If you work for or with institutional asset owners and allocators, involving internal teams and/or external managers (i.e., asset owners/allocators), then this book is a must-read.

Assessing the level of skill possessed by a fund manager is one of the thorniest investment challenges encountered by asset owners/allocators. Whereas earlier in my career we were fortunate in that many of our decisions worked out well, there is no question that my teams and I would have gladly welcomed deeper insights into manager skill—measures like those described in this book. Many of the portfolio metrics commonly used today are more accurately categorized as measures of fund outcomes rather than measures of manager skill, as Mike explains. Nevertheless, analytics such as information ratio, relative return, attribution, and upside/downside capture are relied upon daily to assess manager and fund desirability. A shortcoming of these conventional analytics is that measures of fund outcomes can only hint at the presence or absence of skill. They do not identify or quantify skill directly. This inferential approach to skill analysis can and often does lead to inaccurate manager and fund assessment and disappointing results.

Yet there are a minority of asset owners/allocators who enjoy above-average success in their manager and fund assessments. What these successful asset owners/allocators add to conventional analytics is their extraordinary expert judgments. This is the type of judgment that can bridge the shortcomings of conventional analytics and allow the decision-maker to arrive at the correct interpretation of manager skill. Such judgment is earned through years of fund assessments coupled with rigorous feedback regarding which allocations proved successful, which did not, and all-important reflections on how decisions were arrived at and what could have been done better.

Extraordinary expert judgment is, by definition, not ubiquitous. Assuming that a majority of asset owners/allocators will achieve this level of expertise seems overly optimistic. The question then is how can more asset owners/allocators make better decisions? A big part of the answer, as Mike describes, is the use of better skill metrics. Such metrics would enable a greater number of investment professionals to more effectively differentiate those managers who are highly skilled from those less so. This would support better decisions across the industry while sidestepping the need for more asset owners/allocators to become extraordinarily expert at puzzling together the results from conventional analytics.

In this book, Mike describes a new category of what he terms newer analytics that fit this bill. The fundamental difference between conventional analytics and the newer analytics is the types of data they use. Conventional analytics rely on either a fund's return series or its holdings history to compute their results. In contrast, the newer analytics compute skills based on manager decisions. This seemingly small difference is, in fact, what elevates the newer analytics from mere reflections of skill to the rigorous quantification of skill. As described by the author, the newer analytics capture the cause and effect inherent in generally recognized measures of skill. This includes how skill is defined across sports, jet piloting, surgery, and auto racing, to name but a few examples. Precisely how the newer analytics quantify manager skill is explained in detail throughout the following chapters. These discussions include alternate methods for identifying manager decisions, various techniques for computing skill impacts, and a host of examples based on professionally managed equity funds. Each example illustrates how stronger skill information can help asset owners/allocators make more informed and better decisions.

This book does not shy away from being slightly provocative on a range of topics regarding equity allocations. Explaining the inadequacies of many conventional analytics with regard to skill measurement is one example. Mike also details the uses and misuses of what are sacrosanct concepts, such as William Sharpe's "The Arithmetic of Active Management," Eugene Fama's "efficient market hypothesis," and the industry's general preference for managers who strictly adhere to benchmark compliance and style conformity. Far from questioning today's orthodoxy simply as a heretical exercise, Mike reviews some of today's practices respectfully and offers thoughtful suggestions on how they can be refined to make better choices and achieve stronger portfolio results.

I conclude by referring to the book's initial chapter, which introduces a challenge to asset owners/allocators and other asset management industry participants. We are urged to engage in an industry-wide conversation about skill. This conversation involves rethinking what skill really means, how it should be computed, and the impact better skill metrics can have on allocations and portfolio performance. I believe that the arguments presented in this book for engaging in such a conversation are well reasoned. Moreover, if such a conversation is warranted, there is no better time to commence such an effort than right now.

If we are successful (and yes, a bit lucky) in a handful of years, it may be possible to observe that real skill metrics permeate the asset management industry. If achieved, this outcome will help asset owners/allocators while also benefiting the beneficiaries on whose behalf they toil and the asset management industry generally.

Siew Kai Choy

1 The Search for Skill

The shortcomings of economics are not original error but uncorrected obsolescence. The obsolescence has occurred because what is convenient has become sacrosanct. Anyone who attacks such ideas must seem to be a trifle self-confident and even aggressive.
—John Kenneth Galbraith

The global demand for actively managed equities remains strong, totaling tens of trillions of dollars in assets under management. This demand persists despite the tremendous growth in passively managed equities since 2010. Substantial allocations to actively managed equities are likely to continue for several reasons, including the desire to capture excess returns, securing additional portfolio diversification, and the need to offset individual stock concentration risks embedded in many index tracking passive equity products. Additional motivations for actively managed equity allocations are discussed in chapter 2. The vibrance and ultimate size of this asset class going forward, however, hinges on how confident capital allocators are in their ability to assess equity funds.[1]

Unfortunately, conventional analytics fall short of enabling capital allocators to acquire this ability. These familiar and pervasive analytics do not provide sufficient insight into which managers are highly skilled and which are not, as is taken up in chapter 3. The current knowledge gap impairs the fund assessment process and introduces unnecessary uncertainty that can and should be mitigated. Enhanced skill assessment can help improve individual allocation decisions. It can also provide valuable information as the market continues its search for the most efficient equilibrium point between actively managed and passively managed equities.

Time for Change

Which gets to the purpose of writing this book. It is to begin an industry-wide conversation regarding the nature of skill. What it is? Who has it? How might its consistency be confirmed? This conversation is critically—and urgently—needed, first to debate and then to adopt new ideas about skill analytics. Absent enhanced means for discussing and identifying skill, capital allocators cannot make their best decisions. Nor can the actively managed equities market achieve its full potential while skill remains an enigma. Continuing with the status quo, actively managed equities are destined to continue losing more ground to passive alternatives, very likely beyond the level that best serves investors.

Glimmers of What's Possible

A number of capital allocators have already reenvisioned their fund assessment criteria and processes. This includes the adoption of many of the newer fund analytics described in chapters 4 through 13. These capital allocators have greater confidence in their understanding of the funds with whom they work. Moreover, they are increasingly successful in their fund choices. Unfortunately, at this writing these experiences are few and far between. The vast majority of active equity allocations are being made today based on the incomplete insights provided by conventional analytics. These choices are based on intuition, hunches, and hope as much as objective fund knowledge.

Overcoming Inertia

One reason for the sluggish uptake of the newer analytics surely involves the difficulties surrounding change. Doing things differently is rarely easy. It's even more difficult when an entire industry is organized around analytic concepts that now are ubiquitous, if not sacrosanct. Conventional analytic results are everywhere. They appear in every pitch book. They come up in every meeting between managers and their clients. They are essential elements of every manager assessment process. They are taught in the top business schools and are required components of the exams leading to the chartered financial analyst (CFA) designation. Conventional analytics are valuable for sure. They simply are not sufficient for assessing equity funds or manager skill.

Benefits Beyond Returns

There are many compelling reasons to bring the newer analytics into the mainstream sooner rather than later. Better insights into skill can lead to stronger allocation decisions. This, in turn, can help capital allocators be even more effective in achieving their ultimate goals, whether that involves increasing the distributions available from a sovereign wealth fund, enabling a pension fund to meet the ever-increasing needs of its beneficiaries, expanding the ability of foundations and endowments to achieve their missions, or generally assisting all investors in meeting their financial goals. It is time to radically rethink skill. The more known about skill, the better off all capital allocators are. So let's get the conversation going.

The Skill Gap

Wouldn't it be great to know which equity funds were going to outperform going forward? Of course it would. Unfortunately, this is not possible. It would require predicting the future, which so far doesn't work well. The next best thing, then, is to identify those funds managed by highly skilled experts. The presumption being that, all other things being equal, those managers with the greatest skill are more likely to outperform. Short of delivering excess returns, these elite managers might be expected to at least outperform their less-skilled brethren over time. Such ideas have fueled the decades-long search for skill.

Mountains of research, more than a handful of Nobel Prizes, and scores of analytic techniques lie before the altar of skill identification. Many of these analytics are widely used and now constitute conventional methods for equity fund assessment. These conventional analytics provide tremendous insight into how a fund performed. They also elucidate how the results were achieved, such as by owning the right stocks, allocations to the right sectors, taking concentrated high-conviction bets, and accepting more or less risk. What they don't do—or at least don't do very well—is actually describe skill. They hint at its presence or absence, and that's it. These analytics are incapable of providing meaningful answers to basic questions, such as: What is skill? What does it look like? Are a manager's skills improving, diminishing, or remaining consistent? The shortcomings in our ability to accurately assess or even knowledgeably discuss skills exacerbate the challenges of fund selection and the management of equity allocations.

The Larger Price of Opacity

Weak insights into skill have long defined the public equities industry. Poor feedback about skill makes it virtually impossible for most fund managers to improve, as discussed in my earlier book.[2] This fact, in turn, is largely behind the generally disappointing results from the overall active equity management industry.[3] The lack of knowledge about skill is also why identifying desirable funds is both tremendously difficult and time-consuming. Many capital allocators find the equity fund search to be too burdensome and far too uncertain. These challenges, together with the higher fees associated with active management, have led to an increasing number investing in public equities primarily through low-cost passive products while looking for risk-adjusted excess returns among alternative assets.

Notwithstanding the poor average returns from actively managed equity funds, a sizable number of funds do manage to outperform. And many do it regularly. Identifying which funds have outperformed over the prior one, three, and five years is easy. Finding those that are likely to generate alpha going forward is another matter entirely.[4] Advancing the ability to assess a fund's capacity to provide excess returns tomorrow requires a fresh look at how skill is measured.

Accuracy Versus Meaningful Insight

The principal deterrent to understanding skill is data. Not its availability but the types of data currently used in calculating conventional analytics. For the most part, the data supporting conventional analytics involve return time series or fund holdings histories. These data are well-suited for telling a fund's story with regard to what happened and why. They are perfect for computing return and risk attribution, riskiness, and benchmark divergence. These are not the right data for uncovering which skills actually drove the fund's results. The reason is elemental. Return series and holdings histories are themselves data about fund outcomes. This type of data cannot be reversed to expose meaningful insight into skills, no matter how much it is threatened with mathematical thrashing.

Put simply, skill is not found in the reslicing of outcomes. This is true no matter how exacting or statistically significant the results are. Rather, skill is about understanding decisions. More specifically, skill is identified through connecting how choices made today impact tomorrow's outcomes. There is a cause-and-effect component to skill assessment that is absent in conventional analytics. The void between conventional analytics and real skill metrics can be seen in sports. Knowing how many games a football team (i.e., soccer in the US) has won is useful. If the team wins more than 50% of the games, that is impressive. So, too, is winning more games than most of its peer teams. Yet these outcomes do not tell us about the skill of the team. For that we might want to know about what decisions and actions led to the outcomes, such as: Which players were on the field? How many shots on goal are taken per game? What are the average goals realized per game? And what is the percentage of shots-on-goal by opponents that are deflected? Similarly, the true indicators of equity management skills are found in the decisions and actions taken. The more that is understood about the relationship between decisions and outcomes, the closer we get to truly understanding skill.

Decision Quandary

Precisely what data provides the most efficacious representation of a decision is debatable. On the one hand, it may be as straightforward as a trade. Trade data is readily available, indicates discrete events, and can be mapped to buying, selling, and sizing decisions. On the other hand, there are several approaches that roll up multiple trades in order to express the manager's strategic decisions. Within these latter approaches, trades are viewed as simply the means for implementing the manager's decisions to change the fund composition. Time will tell whether one or more of the current methods for identifying decisions will prevail or if other, even newer techniques will become industry standards. What is of paramount importance is that tremendous progress toward a better understanding of skill can be made right now as this and other technical questions are studied and resolved.

Helpful Background

This book reflects many concepts and ideas I've acquired over years of working in asset management. The most critical of these are below.

Fundamental orientation.   This work is largely focused on the assessment of and allocation to fundamentally managed active equity funds. The ideas and analytics discussed are perfectly suited for quantitatively managed funds and thematically driven funds as well. In fact, the newer analytics are suitable for any publicly traded asset type. Each of the decision-based analytics providers described in chapter 14 works regularly with quantitative, thematic, and fundamental funds.

Target audience.   This book is written with professional capital allocators (i.e., institutional asset owners/allocators) in mind. This will be apparent by the investment terms used, the elaborations (or lack thereof) regarding analytic concepts, the examples presented, and how they are described. Perhaps the most important reason why I've chosen this focus is that after more than four decades both working as an institutional asset manager and developing/marketing analytic products for such professionals, I am writing about what I know best. A second reason is that most of the analytic concepts presented in the following chapters are sufficiently novel that their availability is currently limited to institutional investors. As these analytics become more mainstream, it is likely that elements of them will be incorporated into the many fund ratings services and investment advisory platforms that support the broader investment market. That said, the majority of ideas and concepts discussed herein can be fully appreciated by individual investors and other readers—at least that is the intent.

The title.   You may be wondering about the title *Skill Versus Luck*. I chose it because it is provocative (not a bad quality for a book title) and it reflects the desire behind most manager searches. However, I believe that it presents a false dichotomy. Skill and luck are not binary. A manager or fund does not possess one or the other. Instead, skill and luck lie at alternate ends of a continuum. The more skill a person possesses, the less subject they are to luck and vice versa. The concepts described in this book can help capital allocators to more accurately judge where on this continuum a particular fund or manager resides.

Fund versus manager. I use the terms *fund* and *manager* interchangeably throughout this book. My reasoning is that funds are increasingly being managed by multiple managers, in collaboration with risk and quantitative teams and other decision influencers. Consequently, the notion of a single individual calling all the shots is becoming less and less reality. With more and more technology support (e.g., quantitative models, artificial intelligence, machine learning, large language models), it is increasingly difficult even within fundamental teams to isolate from whom or where the decisions are generated. The term *fund*, therefore, connotes the continued evolution toward human–machine collaborations now managing money.

Alpha shmalpha. Within these pages the term *alpha* refers to its colloquial usage, that being the difference between a fund's returns and those of its benchmark (i.e., relative return). Moreover, to avoid repetition of stupefying proportions you will find that the terms *alpha, excess return, benchmark-beating return, relative return, outperformance,* and *successful outcome* are used synonymously.

No holy grail. This book will not enable you to predict which actively managed equity funds are going to outperform. Not being predictive does not make the newer analytics any less valuable. Consider where equity fund analytics are today. They are neither predictive of future fund results nor do they help significantly in identifying skilled managers. The newer analytics deliver extremely well on the second point: They provide meaningful insights into both manager skills and investment processes. Their results enable capital allocators to be better informed and make better choices. They provide insights regarding which funds have a better-than-average chance of outperforming. That is a lot of value. So, please, let's not get hung up on predictiveness. However, it is likely that others will investigate this topic over time.

The decision fallacy. We don't arrive at decisions the way we think we do. My beliefs on this topic can be distilled to these three points:

1. Most decisions (about 95%) are made unconsciously. They are formed with little or no conscious deliberation. This fact has all sorts of implications. One important one to remember is that what we say are our reasons for making a choice are frequently stories our unconscious provides after the fact. This bit of self-storytelling helps us feel in control and have confidence in our choices (even when it is unwarranted).

2. Biased decisions are commonplace. Biases are constructed from faulty learnings that then help form unfounded beliefs. Identical to how we make decisions largely unconsciously, so too we frequently learn and retain information without conscious involvement. Faulty learning and biases impact financial decisions through a variety of mental processes, including heuristics, rules-of-thumb, and intuitions.

3. Emotions are essential for rational decision-making. OK, I get that this may seem blasphemous to some of you. It is in direct conflict with prevailing notions such as *Homo economicus*, the rational actor, and the perpetually wealth maximizing decision maker. I am all for the use of these constructs when explaining an economic model. But I draw the line at pretending that any of us actually behave this way. Real decision-making is full of emotional content. Hope, anxiety, fear, and desire are as integral to financial decisions as are numbers. With the exception of market sentiment, however, discussions within asset management about emotions are avoided like the plague. You'll find references to varying types of emotional forces throughout the following chapters.

Conclusion

Enormous levels of capital are invested in actively managed equities. While interest in this asset class remains strong, the portion of equities that will remain actively managed is uncertain. What is clear is that the future size of this asset class is inextricably linked to the level of confidence developed by capital allocators in identifying manager skill.

Currently used conventional analytics are helpful in understanding a fund's past performance. They also are suggestive of fund skill. These analytics, however, are not able to clearly identify which skills are driving fund results. Nor can they quantify the impacts of various skills on excess fund returns. The absence of rigorous skill information impedes fund assessment processes and diminishes the potential for this asset class.

Fortunately, there are newer analytics that actually quantify skill. The newer analytics directly relate manager decisions to fund outcomes. These decision-based skill analytics provide rigorous and granular insights into how effectively a fund buys, sells, and sizes stocks. Newer analytics provide the means to explore both the magnitude and persistence of skills. These newer analytics are being used today by capital allocators to help make stronger allocation decisions.

The balance of this book describes how the newer analytics work and how they zero in on distinct skills. My hope is that the concepts and analytics presented will help to ignite the much-needed conversation within asset management regarding skill. Specifically, this industry conversation needs to address the following questions: What does skill look like? How best can it be quantified? How can capital allocators use newer skill metrics to make more effective allocation decisions? And how can these same analytics be used to help fund managers learn and improve?

Now on to the discussion of skill.

2   Sage Advice

By three methods we may learn wisdom: First, by reflection, which is noblest; second, by imitation, which is easiest; and third, by experience, which is the bitterest.
—Confucius

I wanted to understand more about what capital allocators are thinking about actively managed equities. This led me to speak with senior executives representing a host of organizations, including sovereign wealth funds, foundations, pension funds, endowments, outsourced chief investment officers (OCIO), as well as search consultants, asset managers, university professors, providers of skill assessment software, and other industry service providers (the contributors). These conversations were highly informative. What quickly became clear is that many top capital allocators are bullish on actively managed equities. They are able to invest profitably in this asset class—meaning that across a diverse group of external (and sometimes internal) funds, their sets of active equity allocations generate excess returns more often than not. Given their levels of success with this asset class, these capital allocators anticipate maintaining their allocations to actively managed equities going forward.

Having completed these conversations, I then pondered how best to present the insights obtained in a concise and informative manner. Rather than using the familiar question-and-answer construct, I chose to report on what I learned as a series of discussion topics. Each observation includes wisdom synthesized from conversations with multiple contributors. This approach facilitates capturing a variety of perspectives on each theme while avoiding repetition. Each idea expressed includes the extensive experiences of several contributors gained from collectively managing trillions of dollars of active equities over multiple decades. Both the intellectual rigor and strong grounding in practical asset management of the contributors is readily evident. A list of the contributors is provided in the acknowledgments.

It was a privilege having the opportunity to speak with these individuals. They are all highly regarded experts in their respective fields. Moreover, they were not only gracious with their time and knowledge but speaking with each was truly a pleasure. In doing my best to faithfully represent what they have taught me, I hope to express my deep appreciation for their kindness and support in this endeavor.

Theory, Folklore, and Practice

Asset management reflects a wide range of theories, hypotheses, and analytics. When applied correctly, they can frequently guide capital allocators to successful choices. Their misapplication or motivated interpretation, however, can quickly lead to unfounded conclusions, weak decisions, and unintended consequences. It's what happens when hunches and hope are unknowingly substituted for knowledge and facts.

The good news is that many capital allocators are now conducting their actively managed equity fund assessments in a much more rigorous fashion. This includes approaches that are steeped in the appropriate financial theories, conducted with meaningful analytic input, and performed within a highly disciplined process. The idea of such a decision framework is by no means novel. What's new is how it is being implemented. Key among the many refinements is the willingness to rethink the industry's folklore. This includes the desire to separate out from tradition what's actually helpful and under what conditions. And then think anew as to what concepts and analytics can provide stronger insights. Highlights of how fund assessment is morphing are presented below. Any errors or misstatements are the sole property of the author.

Sharpe's Mathematics Revisited

In 1991 William Sharpe wrote what has become an important paper in finance, "The Arithmetic of Active Management."[1] Sharpe lays out a straightforward argument for why the majority of actively managed capital will underperform, particularly when fees and expenses are taken into account. The crux of Sharpe's proposition, in his own words, is as follows:

> If "active" and "passive" management styles are defined in sensible ways, it must be the case that (1) before costs, the return on the average actively managed dollar will equal the return on the average passively managed dollar and (2) after costs, the return on the average actively managed dollar will be less than the return on the average passively managed dollar.

Champions of passive or index investing seem well familiar with this passage. It is frequently referenced as the definitive repudiation of active management. It certainly puts active management in a dismal light, absent any further context.

Further on in this same paper, however, Sharpe goes on to say:

> This need not be taken as a counsel of despair. It is perfectly possible for some active managers to beat their passive brethren, even after costs. Such managers must, of course, manage a minority share of the actively managed dollars within the market in question. It is also possible for an investor (such as a pension fund) to choose a set of active managers that, collectively, provides a total return better than that of a passive alternative, even after costs. Not all the managers in the set have to beat their passive counterparts, only those managing a majority of the investor's actively managed funds.

This second observation from Sharpe is rarely, if ever, mentioned by passive enthusiasts. Its omission precludes the thoughtful discussion regarding when and how actively managed equities can be beneficial. Furthermore, the out-and-out dismissal of actively managed equities is not in the best interest of many investors. A great number of capital allocators recognize that they are not destined to purchase only the average active returns. Instead, they are seeking out and finding those managers that possess sufficient skill so that they can generate excess returns more often than not. As one contributor put it: "What we're interested in are the elite managers. Those with the skills to generate alpha." This individual likened it to tennis: "Not every weekend player gets to compete at Wimbledon. It's only for the elite players. These are the same sort of criteria we're applying to identify equity managers."

The point is that Sharpe's analysis is not the anti-active management manifesto that it sometimes is held out to be. It is for sure a sobering analysis of why the majority of actively managed capital will underperform. Yet it is very clear that there are options other than investing in the average performing (i.e., underperforming) fund. Specifically, Sharpe says in no uncertain terms that it is possible to construct a set of actively managed allocations that can generate excess returns. This is, in fact, being done now by a variety of sophisticated capital allocators on a global basis.

Imperfect Information

Another argument against actively managed equities comes from the efficient market hypothesis (EMH), largely attributed to Eugene Fama.[2] The essence of EMH suggests that the same information is generally available at the same time to all market participants. Therefore, it is unlikely that sustainable outperformance can be achieved through the identification of unique and valuable insights regarding stock mispricing. EMH is widely regarded as an important analytic framework for conceptualizing behavior within an efficient market. There are questions, however, concerning how completely it represents the dynamics observable within actual markets such as equities.

It can be argued that with some combination of highly expert fundamental research, quantitative alpha seeking models, and artificial intelligence tools, a manager can formulate an insight about a stock well before others or at least before most others. To the extent that this is true, then it means that these individuals can trade on knowledge that is proprietary or not yet priced into the market—at least for some period of time. Such unique and valuable insights are what is meant by the idea of a manager's information advantage.

As one contributor suggests: "One question that needs to be addressed is, are markets perfectly transparent or are they imperfect? If they are perfect, then the likelihood of being a successful active manager is grim. Everyone knows what you know and can act as easily. A perfect market is a strong argument for going passive. On the other hand, if the market is imperfect, then it is possible to arrive at insights ahead of others or to have insights that are simply different from others. This suggests opportunity. This opens the door for active management."[3]

Vast amounts of information are both broadly available and instantly accessible. The question, then, is whether it is possible to add value to this information through the application of hard-won experience, expertise, creative synthesis of old and new ideas, and disciplined effort. The fact that a great number of capital allocators continue to rely upon and generate excess returns from actively managed equities points to the answer being in the affirmative.

Rethinking the Benchmark Relationship

Information asymmetry is fundamental to active management. Without it, alpha from stock selection seems improbable, if not downright impossible. The ability to capitalize on information asymmetries relates directly to the flexibility in fund construction or degrees of freedom available to the manager. The more benchmark-constrained a fund's mandate, the fewer degrees of freedom. It's that straightforward. The search for alpha is exacerbated as benchmark total weights become ever more skewed toward a handful or so of mega stocks.[4] Manager time and fund capital committed to conforming with tracking error and attribution constraints ultimately limit what can be owned and the size of active positions. What are intended as reasonable guardrails can become unintentional barriers to generating excess returns.

Some capital allocators are choosing to give greater latitude to individual equity funds. This translates into allowing the funds to be a bit more concentrated, varying the weights of holdings significantly from their reference indices, and even to own positions outside of their benchmarks. These funds then have the degrees of freedom to show what they can do—ideally, pick great stocks. These same capital allocators then manage their equity risks at the aggregate or portfolio level. This is where composite under- and overexposures, together with market regime changes, can be identified and ameliorated effectively. Since risk management is a skill at which most capital allocators (or their consultants) excel, this approach can be both highly productive and very efficient.

Importantly, this approach still facilitates meaningful assessment of each allocation. The funds' returns can be compared to those of its benchmark to evaluate overall performance. Additionally, the returns of individual stocks purchased by the fund can be compared to the median returns of their benchmark sectors. This sector-relative comparison helps in assessing if the fund is buying from among the best stocks in each sector (an interesting adjunct to skill quantification). The benefit of this approach, as many perceive it, is that allocations continue to have specific roles within the overall portfolio (defined by style and benchmark) while redirecting managers away from so-called benchmark hugging and instead focusing their decisions on owning the strongest stocks available within their investable universes.

The use of this allocation approach is far from widespread. More common today are allocations to funds that are expected to deliver it all—excess returns, low volatility, a reasonable risk profile, strong upside capture, and downside protection. In order to try and meet these broad if not conflicting expectations, fund construction invariably moves ever closer to mirroring its benchmark. This means that, within many funds, the search for alpha regularly takes a back seat to risk management. The result is a mash-up of bold desires followed by timid allocations—an approach that makes it difficult to build a successful active equity program.

The higher degrees of freedom approach to fund allocations may not be suitable for every size and form of capital allocator. Many allocators do not actively manage composite risks and exposures. They make wise allocation decisions and then expect each fund to do its part in managing risk. Currently, the higher degrees of freedom approach is being used not only by sophisticated asset owners but also by builders of multiasset products and separately managed accounts. Improving analytic technology, together with the ability to more effectively identify skilled equity funds, may help this approach gain greater traction sooner than later.

Great Funds Do Exist

Identifying funds that are more likely than not to outperform remains a sizable challenge. Heartening to this search process is increasing information on the number of funds that regularly outperform (i.e., elite funds). An excellent source of research in this regard is the software and services firm Inalytics Ltd. Inalytics has applied their proprietary skill analysis software to approximately 1,200 actively managed equity funds. Their research findings show that 88% of the funds analyzed beat their respective benchmarks (generated alpha) for five years or more; the mean excess return was 3.97% annualized across those with positive alpha; and the vast majority (90% or so) of the alpha was generated through strong buying or what Inalytics refers to as "the research process," whereas the sizing skill, or choosing which positions to make large or small weights, had virtually no impact or detracted modestly from fund results.[5] Based on their extensive work,

Inalytics suggests that "Asset Owners ought to spend an amount of time and effort understanding the efficacy of the research process commensurate to its importance when carrying out their due diligence on prospective managers." Inalytics' results are based on $1.2 trillion in assets under management and more than $7.4 trillion in asset trades.

FactSet-Cabot, another leading skill analytics provider, offers a similar perspective into fund outperformance and skill assessment. This company has analyzed in excess of 600 long-only equity funds. Approximately 60% of these funds were outperforming at the time they were initially analyzed. The reason for the difference in outperforming versus underperforming funds encountered by FactSet-Cabot versus Inalytics is not completely clear. It is possible that, at least to some extent, the higher percentage of underperforming funds in the FactSet-Cabot data reflects this company's historic orientation toward helping fund managers improve. This may have led to more troubled funds seeking the services of FactSet-Cabot in hopes of regaining past levels of success.

Consistent with the Inalytics research, the FactSet-Cabot research results show that strong buying underpins outperforming funds. The FactSet-Cabot results indicate that the buy skill tends to add between 100 and 600 basis points of annual alpha across the outperforming funds. Sizing was a slight negative contributor to results across all of the funds analyzed. It was further observed that interim trading (trims and adds) has a negative contribution to fund returns in three-quarters of all funds analyzed. Whereas approximately one-half of funds add to excess returns with their initial position sizing (i.e., weight established soon after initial purchase). Finally, two-thirds of all funds analyzed by FactSet-Cabot lost alpha from ineffective selling decisions. This includes selling winners too quickly (before their full alpha is captured), holding on to losers as they continue to spiral downward, and allowing older winners that had become tired to linger in the fund rather than recycle their capital.

While not exhaustive in scope, these two sets of results point to a significant number of actively managed funds that possess the skill and capacity to generate alpha. Understandably, some will criticize these two fund groups as not being representative of the industry at large. They'll mention how skewed the funds are toward outperformers. Such pundits would be correct, of course. But they'd also be missing the point. The fact that the majority of all actively managed equity funds underperform is old news.

What's not as well appreciated is that there are many funds that actually outperform and do so regularly. It was Sharpe himself who suggested that some number of funds can outperform. Now there is evidence that these funds really do exist.

Outperformance is found among the elite funds. And the groups described thus far by no means contain all or the majority of funds capable of generating excess returns consistently. Three other skill analytics providers—Alpha Theory, Behaviour Lab, and Essentia Analytics—have also identified elite fund managers.[6] In aggregate these five firms have analyzed thousands of equity funds, many of which are generating alpha consistently.

There are indeed elite funds, as Sharpe suggested. These elite funds don't deliver average results. They generate alpha and do it consistently. Elite funds exist throughout the active product lineup, including mutual funds, electronically traded funds, comingled institutional funds, separately managed accounts, exclusive internally managed funds, and more. These are elite funds that capital allocators can work with today. And as more and more capital allocators integrate newer analytics and more disciplined processes into their fund assessments, this activity will create a favorable feedback loop. Funds will realize they must explain their skills and processes, not just their results. The types of information used will be refined over time and become more readily available. As the newer analytics and measures of skills mature, their use will expand to supporting ever more capital allocators, investment advisors, and individual or retail investors. These same metrics may then become part of fund management itself and enable more elite funds to emerge. And while not every fund can outperform (a tip of the hat to Mr. Sharpe), there is at present plenty of room for many more funds to regularly deliver alpha.

The Importance of Time Horizon

Skilled fundamental stock decisions unfold over many months and frequently several years. Assessing skill repeatability, therefore, requires multiples of these timeframes. Yet tremendous amounts of energy are invested in analyzing the short-term results of equity funds. There is no question that a lot can be learned from recent results. A strong quarter or two may indicate that a fund is continuing to perform as hoped for or even improving. By contrast, weakening results might suggest a possible skill erosion that needs to be carefully watched. Unfortunately, the temptation to overly interpret or overreact to short-term results is powerful. This is especially true when allocations are made based upon an inadequate understanding of a fund's skills, investment processes, and potential for repeatability.

Fragile and incomplete knowledge concerning a fund's capabilities enables positive or negative news to undermine allocation decisions. In such situations hope and fear can run roughshod over analytic thinking. A short-listed fund might move up to allocation status in response to extremely strong recent results. Similarly, a fund that yesterday was a buy or hold can quickly become a sell after a few quarters of disappointing returns. One needs only look at fund flows after a year of relatively strong or weak performance for confirmation of such actions. While this behavior may be more pronounced among individual investors, capital allocators are no strangers to this type of short-termism. Taking a longer view, as recommended by seasoned capital allocators, can mitigate overresponding to short-term results. Even the very best funds have off years, sometimes even a string of them. Having the internal fortitude to stay with an allocation that is experiencing a temporary headwind can pay off handsomely. This is particularly true when the appropriate analytics confirm that the fund's skills and investment processes have not eroded—auguring well for the likelihood of a turnaround in results. As one contributor indicated: "Taking a longer time horizon is actually one of our competitive advantages."

The specific types of stocks purchased by a fund represent another important time element. One fund may make great buys that begin to take off soon after purchase and then approach exhaustion in twelve to fifteen months. Another fund with the same mandate might regularly buy stocks that show no or little signs of life for four or more months. Then these late starters might slowly begin to grow and ultimately hit their full stride twelve or eighteen months after purchase, continuing to compound for months thereafter. A solid understanding of how each fund buys and how its typical stock generates alpha over time helps in gauging results over the correct timeframe and mustering the appropriate patience.

Rethinking Style

Style analysis is yet another innovation of William Sharpe.[7] Commonly referred to as return-based or top-down style analysis, Sharpe's style analysis is used to explain the sources of a fund's results based on the factor exposures of its holdings, such as growth/value, small/large capitalization, and high/low price momentum. An alternative bottom-up or holdings-based method of style analysis that was introduced in the early 1990s uses details about each position held in a fund to determine its style. Notwithstanding the complexities associated with assigning style characteristics to a fund or its individual holdings, both methods offer useful insights into the sources of past results.[8]

Where style analysis seems to go awry is when it is used to dictate how a fund should operate. Such overuse begins with the assignment of each fund to one of several so-called style boxes or categories. Allocators then select funds to diversify their investments across various style categories. The expectation is that styles will come into and out of favor over time. The hope is that allocating to a variety of styles will dampen the effects of market cyclicality. In this application, the style of each fund has both a risk management and alpha generation purpose. When style is used as a risk management tool it is expected by the capital allocator that positions held by the fund will remain style consistent. While style consistency across positions may help allocators with their risk management, doing so comes at the direct expense of generating excess returns.

Consider a highly successful value fund that purchases a single new stock each month, gives it an equal (pro rata) size upon purchase, and then sells it after one year. On average, new buys reflect clear value characteristics at purchase and for the initial three months after. Then, beginning in month four, they begin to experience positive price momentum and other indicators of growth. By month six or seven, the typical new buy is relatively growthy and its price continues to climb until it is sold. Which means that at any point in time the vast majority of positions held are more growth than value, most of the fund's capital is invested in growthier positions, and the fund's returns are being driven more by growth stocks than value stocks. Style analysis applied to one or more years of history for this fund would not place it in a value box. It might come out as core, blend, or possibly having a growth tilt. Yet each and every stock when purchased is unquestionably a value stock. Which raises the question: Is this a value fund or not?

In order for this fund to maintain its value designation as conventionally defined, it would need to sell its winners sooner, trim the winners aggressively, or do both and then redeploy this capital back into value stocks. This would keep most of the capital invested in positions with clear value characteristics. It would also cause the fund to forgo a significant amount of alpha or stock appreciation. Does this make economic sense? The answer is plainly no. Yet it is precisely how a large portion of the industry works. Capital allocators frequently forgo the capture of incremental alpha by requiring that the funds they've allocated to minimize style drift. In these situations, the capital allocator uses style to help implement their overall risk management. The result is that many funds manage their holdings to remain within a style box in deference to striving for excess returns. A vivid example of how style adherence can result in unintended consequences is presented in chapter 10 (see figure 10.4).

Fortunately, it is possible to use style in the allocation process and also capture the full alpha from a fund's best buys. It involves evaluating the fund's new buys with respect to its style designation. That's it. A value fund would be expected to purchase value stocks, a growth fund would buy growth stocks, and a small cap fund would buy small capitalization stocks. Confirming this is easily done with some form of purchase context analysis, such as that discussed in chapter 8. Once the stocks are purchased, however, the goal then shifts more toward maximizing alpha.[9] This means that value stocks that grow wildly do not need to be pruned or sold quickly. Similarly, small cap stocks that go on a growth tear can be held longer to capture more of their price appreciation. Within this regime style analysis is used to assess that the fund is buying what is intended, no more. After their purchase, the fund's holdings are then managed with an eye toward alpha generation rather than style conformity (at least more so than today). Naturally, there is room in this approach for construction parameters that limit the riskiness of a fund. Conventional style analysis can continue to be used where it delivers useful insights—post hoc assessment of how fund results were achieved. This is yet another way that managers are being provided expanded degrees of freedom as they seek excess returns.

A Look at Retail

Actively managed equities remain attractive to individual or retail investors. Demand may even be growing. Renewed interest here reflects lower costs and newer product structures.

The average actively managed mutual fund fee has come down considerably over the past two decades. It is no coincidence that active fees declined as allocations to low-cost passive products skyrocketed. Actively managed electronically traded funds (ETF) are now delivering active results at fees considerably lower than their mutual fund counterparts. This is likely to keep active mutual fund fees in check, if not result in further downward pressure. Advisors continue to lower the costs of their services as well. Long gone are the days when advisors were compensated by expensive fund loads. The majority now earn their fees as a percentage of client assets. This has resulted in a better alignment between the financial interests of the advisor and the client. This newer fee structure has also encouraged competition based on price. More recently, some advisors are charging a fixed fee for basic investment advice and additional fees for bespoke services, such as constructing separately managed accounts (SMA), assistance with establishing trusts and wills, and other services. Alignment with large investment platform providers enables advisors to deliver increasingly sophisticated investment solutions while also allowing them to maintain lean operations. Lower costs all around are helping to keep actively managed equities an attractive option for retail investors.

ETF products, in comparison to mutual funds, provide investors with greater liquidity and tax advantages. Some ETF products are based upon higher concentration funds (in sync with the alpha generating commentary above). The SMA product is also growing in popularity. According to one contributor: "Active managers have lots of opportunity within the SMA structure." This is facilitated by the use of advanced portfolio construction/ risk management tools. "You can start with an overall fee target and a risk limit. Then the technology resolves on an optimal mix of passive and active products for a specific type of client." The higher the ratio of alpha-to-cost available from actively managed equities, the greater will be their allocations within these optimized investment solutions.

Lower costs, more attractive products, and the growing sophistication of portfolio construction technology are enabling retail investors to capture many of the opportunities long available to institutional investors. Within this more investor-favorable environment, actively managed equities can serve retail investors well, especially as such products remain cost-competitive and the identification of elite funds becomes easier.

Conclusion

Actively managed equities remain an attractive asset class for capital allocators. Many are able to regularly achieve excess returns from their carefully constructed set of external (and internal) funds. What separates the
experiences of these capital allocators from many of their peers is that they
approach the allocation process with fresh thinking regarding what they
want from equity managers and how to assess manager skill. Across a series
of conversations with contributors representing a wide range of expertise,
several themes emerged regarding how capital allocators are rethinking their
strategies and processes.

Many capital allocators recognize that they can do better than invest with
merely average funds. They comb the industry for elite funds that can deliver
excess returns in more years than not. The right combination of such funds
enables these capital allocators to consistently capture alpha from their overall actively managed equity programs.

These capital allocators understand that top managers build and maintain
an information advantage. This advantage enables such managers to identify
alpha generating stocks regularly. These capital allocators also recognize that
fund managers can deliver their best when they are able to operate with the
greatest degrees of freedom. This has translated into placing less emphasis
on comparing a fund's holdings with its benchmark. Instead, managers are
expected to buy great stocks (without engaging in excessive risks). Capital
allocators may then manage overall active equity risk exposures at the composite or portfolio level.

Analytic results across thousands of funds make it clear that elite managers exist. These managers generate benchmark-beating returns more often
than not. They do it primarily with skilled buying. Understanding a manager's skill in buying and the consistency of their buy process is increasingly
essential information for fund assessment.

Once an allocation is made, it is important to assess its ongoing success over a reasonable timeframe. The majority of high-performing fundamental funds reflect an information advantage that can take twelve
months, twenty-four months, or more for new buys to deliver their full
potential. Knowledge of a fund's information advantage together with the
appreciation that even elite funds will encounter periods of underperformance is leading some capital allocators to embrace longer horizons for

fund evaluations. This is perhaps one of the toughest challenges given the short-term scrutiny that capital allocators endure. Developing a deeper knowledge of each fund's skills and investment processes and sharing this information with boards of directors and other governance bodies can help to better align expectations with results.

Style analysis, while highly useful, can be an obstruction to alpha generation. Although style analysis provides helpful insights into how a fund generated its returns, it can put the brakes on alpha generation when used to restrict ongoing fund composition. Rethinking how style can be used to ensure that a fund is buying the types of stocks intended versus restricting what it can own offers important latitude for fund alpha generation.

Finally, retail investors are reawakening to the benefits of actively managed equities. Lower fees and smarter product offerings are enabling these investors to realize a more attractive dollar of return per dollar of fee than ever before. Optimized investment solutions provided by large asset management companies and investment advisory services allow retail investors to achieve the right level of actively managed equity exposure for their unique investment objectives (e.g., returns, risks, expenses, and time horizon). As newer analytics become more prevalent, they will find their way into generally available fund ratings products and other screening systems.

3 Looking for Skill in All the Wrong Places

The world we have created is a product of our thinking; it cannot be changed without changing our thinking.
—Albert Einstein

Equity fund selection today relies heavily on conventional portfolio analytics. These metrics are used extensively to understand past fund performance. They also underpin searches for skilled managers by all manner of professional investor. They are relied upon by various institutional capital owners and allocators (e.g., sovereign wealth funds, pension schemes, foundations, endowments, banks, insurance companies), asset aggregators (e.g., funds of funds, life cycle funds), and independent fiduciaries (e.g., family offices, search consultants, outsourced chief investment officers), collectively referred to throughout this book as "capital allocators." Unfortunately, the current practice of fund selection is not as effective as believed to be or desired by capital allocators. The reason is that conventional analytics, while enormously helpful in assessing fund returns, construction, and risk, fall well short of actually identifying or measuring manager skill. Overreliance on these metrics surely has led to drawing erroneous conclusions regarding manager skill as well as subpar allocations. Making more effective allocations begins with changing how the industry thinks about manager skill. In particular this involves shifting away from measures of outcome as proxies of skill and focusing on the decisions managers make that drive outcomes.

Industry Best Practices

Currently, capital allocators looking for skilled managers rely upon a host of analytics developed since the 1950s. These conventional analytics generate

myriad metrics that accurately describe a variety of fund results and construction characteristics. Among the most widely used conventional analytics
are relative return, tracking error, information ratio, attribution, upside/
downside capture, multifactor alpha, hit rates, active share, batting average,
slugging ratio, and risk. These and other metrics offer tremendous insights
into how a fund has performed recently and over time. They also provide
insights into how such fund performance was generated (e.g., through risk
exposures, style tilts, position concentration, benchmark divergence, and
more). As this collection of conventional analytics flourished, many were
heralded not only as better explainers of fund results but indicators (if not
measures) of manager skill. In fact, many of these analytics did provide useful
incremental information regarding the sources and quality of fund results.
The knowledge gained from these analytics addresses important allocation
decisions.

For example, style analysis not only makes it possible to understand how
a fund is actually investing, it also supports the intentional diversification
across funds (i.e., different sources of alpha). Attribution analysis explains
the drivers of a fund's past excess return with regard to stock selection, sector
allocation, and factor exposures. These results help explain how the fund is
generating its excess return (or not). The many risk models now available
shed light on the level of comparative volatility and factor exposures being
undertaken by a fund compared with its benchmark or peer group in order
to generate its returns. Active share characterizes the extent to which a
fund's generation of excess returns rests on the success of a handful of large
holdings or a greater number of smaller sized active weights. It's arguable
that these metrics also provide a glimpse of likely skill (or its absence). But
not much more than a glimpse. Yet these metrics are routinely employed
as indicators of manager skill. And although they are unquestionably necessary for understanding fund performance and composition characteristics,
they are not sufficient for assessing skill. In all likelihood their limitations
regarding skill quantification have exacerbated the challenges facing active
manager selection. This means that capital allocators may unknowingly be
lured into believing that they possess more insights into manager skill than
is possible from these analytic measures.

The shortcomings of conventional metrics as measures of skill stem mostly
from the data types used in their calculations. Historical return series, together
with fund holdings and their weights, are what drive these analytics. Such

data work well in assessing historical fund returns and construction charac-teristics. They are rich in insights about how a fund performed and why and where its performance deviated from its benchmark or peer group. What these data lack is the ability to explain which of the manager's decisions are consistently helping to generate excess returns and which are not. While metrics based on these data can be used to infer the presence or absence of skill, this is a highly imprecise, if not downright risky, endeavor. Mea-sures of outcome, no matter how thoughtfully conceived, are insufficient for effectively identifying and quantifying skill. Before venturing further into reviewing conventional analytics it is useful to consider how skill is described currently and what might be a better definition for manager skill.

Got Skill?

Manager skill is undoubtedly the most popular topic of discussion across active equity investing. Concern regarding who, if anyone, has skill domi-nates manager search efforts, internal investment committee meetings, conference panel discussions, academic articles, and the financial press. Yet just what is meant by the term *skill* is neither well understood nor generally agreed upon. The prevailing assumption seems to be that skill is present when a fund generates excess returns or alpha. More precisely, it is believed that if a fund outperforms its benchmark, it's because the manager is skilled and vice versa. While such a tautology may be intuitively appealing, it is both incomplete and misguiding.

Consider this example. A tennis player possesses tremendous ability at serving and at hitting ground strokes. The majority of them go precisely where they are intended, and many are not returned by opponents—meaning they win points. This individual is clearly skilled at hitting serves and ground strokes. This same player's volley game is a very different story. The player's game falls apart at the net. The volleys are weak and easily returned—often resulting in lost points. Overall, their net game is suffi-ciently weak that it causes the player to lose more games than are won. Losing more than 50% of games is tantamount to a fund being below its benchmark. Yet, although this player is not winning as many games as desired, it's abundantly clear that they are skilled. Just not sufficiently skilled to win more than half of the games played. Ergo, while an abun-dance of skill can lead to successful outcomes, outcomes themselves are not clear indicators of the presence or absence of skill. This is true for tennis, other sports, most professions, and especially equity management.

There's plenty of evidence that a fund run by a highly skilled manager can underperform for two, three, or more years in a row. It happens regularly. Similarly, a fund managed by someone of limited skill can outperform for multiple years. This latter manager may benefit from a significant style tailwind or a handful of fortunate stock purchases (think the "Magnificent Seven" of 2023–2024). And therein lies the rub in using outcomes and metrics derived from such data as proxies for skill: They are inferential indicators and not true skill measures. The generation of false positives or false negatives is far more likely than landing on the truth. Both false assessments are highly problematic. They exacerbate the uncertainty surrounding fund assessment and heighten the perceived riskiness of equity investing. Reliance on conventional analytics is a likely contributor to the unfavorable perceptions regarding actively managed equities relative to many other asset types. This possibility further underscores why the industry is very much in need of a better definition for skill, one that makes possible the true identification and quantification of skill.

Defining Skill

A good definition for skill should meet several basic requirements: It should support the computation of rigorous and granular values, rely on readily available data, and encourage adoption through its simplicity and intuitive appeal. With these criteria in mind, I proffer the following definition:

Definition: Skill is the combined effect of expert judgment and investment processes.

Let's consider this definition a bit. The first point to observe is that its two independent terms are entirely in the control of the manager. Professionals can unquestionably enhance their expert judgment as well as refine their investment processes. In contrast, a manager cannot completely control fund outcomes. That's because outcomes depend upon judgment and process for sure but also on luck (noncontrollable market dynamics). The skill portion (judgment and process) is what the manager brings to the fund and what the manager should be evaluated upon. A second point is that this proposed definition uses the phrase "combined effects" for good reason. Although measuring the impacts of judgment and process as distinctly as possible is preferred, it may not be 100% achievable. Nevertheless, identifying where judgment, process, and their combined effects result in successful and unsuccessful decisions goes a long way toward quantifying manager skill.

This approach provides much more clarity about skill than is possible from relying solely on measures of fund outcomes (i.e., conventional analytics). Newer analytics based on this definition can answer important questions, such as:

- Does the manager possess a clear information advantage? And if so, is it being fully captured?
- Are the excess returns provided by new buys over time remaining steady, getting stronger, or weakening?
- Are the fund's winners being brought up to full weight in a timely fashion, or is alpha being lost due to sluggish buildup of position size?
- Are older winners being harvested effectively or allowed to linger in the fund well past their productive lives?
- Are substantial losers being managed skillfully, or are they regularly destroying capital and lowering fund results?
- Do the stocks the manager buys reflect a consistent process (factor signature), or are they more opportunistic and varied in their character?

Answers to questions like these can provide rigorous and granular insights into skill—its presence, its magnitude, and its consistency. It's the kind of information that can meaningfully improve the fund assessment and allocation process. It can provide capital allocators with greater conviction in their allocation decisions and guide them toward capturing more alpha.[1] Given these new thoughts about the nature of skill within equity management, the discussion now returns to further exploring the strengths and shortcomings of conventional analytics.

Stretching the Facts

Absent direct measures of skill, the industry has been using the available analytics to their fullest and then some. Going well beyond the calculations of past performance, risk, and fund construction, conventional analytics are regularly relied upon as indicators of skill. One possible reason for this extended use may be that in addition to these metrics making intuitive sense, it may be presumed that if several conventional analytics are used together, the combined answer affords a reasonable approximation of skill. Another possible reason is that conventional metrics are, for the most part, the creation of highly regarded academics. Such august heritage may bestow sufficient credibility that as each conventional analytic is introduced, it is presumed to be a good indicator of skill and then readily adopted by practitioners for this purpose. Of course, some of the academic studies themselves have encouraged the overinterpretation of these metrics. Although these studies measured the correlation of various metrics with fund excess returns, their results were occasionally presented as identifying causality (i.e., measures of skill).[2]

Yet another reason may be emotional. The unconscious desire to corral nagging doubts and move forward with conviction is powerful, even if such conviction rests on weak underpinnings. Individual capital allocators may unknowingly want the results of conventional analytics to be good enough proxies for skill so that they can be relied upon when assessing a fund. To the extent this behavior exists, it is consistent with a mental processing framework referred to as motivated reasoning. The thrust of this framework is that emotions (e.g., fear and desire) often overwhelm analytic thinking. The upshot being choices or conclusions that are experienced as the culmination of objective deliberation but which are, in fact, partially or largely the answers needed to satisfy a desire or avoid psychic pain.[3] Attempting to identify which manager among several is more likely than their peers to generate excess returns going forward is ultimately a judgment call. Doing it based on the results from conventional analytics alone is likely to provoke angst in even the most stoic of capital allocators.

It is impossible to sort out for sure how much of an investment decision relies on analytic thinking and how much is motivated by unconscious desires. What is clear is that conventional analytics are often misinterpreted and misapplied. The consequence is the unintended misuse of their results leading to poor allocation decisions. Descriptions of how several commonly used analytics can lead to inaccurate assessments of skill are provided next.

Attribution

Basic attribution analysis computes how much of a fund's excess returns are the result of stock selection versus sector allocation. Both measures reflect the fund's returns relative to a benchmark and the overweighting and underweighting of positions within sectors. Positive return from stock selection indicates that, for individual sectors, the manager overweighted stocks that outperformed their sector average and/or underweighted stocks that underperformed their sector average. The opposite would be true for negative return from stock selection. Positive return from sector selection signifies that the manager overweighted sectors that outperformed the benchmark and/or underweighted sectors that underperformed the benchmark.[4] Positive return from stock selection is easily misconstrued as indicating that the manager is skilled at buying stocks. The relationship between return from stock selection and buy skill is, however, tenuous at best. Befuddlement regarding this relationship may be due in part to nomenclature. Taken literally, the term "stock selection" can be misconstrued to refer to the act of selecting stocks to purchase. With regard to attribution, however, the word "selection" does not refer to buying. Instead, it refers to which stocks the manager chooses (or selects) to hold in the fund during the time period analyzed. Some of the fund's positions may in fact have been purchased during the period being examined. Other positions may have been purchased at the very beginning of the analysis time frame or several months or years prior to the start of the analysis period. Moreover, for any one year of fund history, the average age of all positions held might be as low as ten months (i.e., high turnover fund) or as high as multiple years (i.e., low turnover fund). Consequently, while return from stock selection may be slightly more reflective of buy skill in a high turnover fund, this metric incorporates the results of more decisions than just buying. Return from stock selection also reflects the unique weights given to various positions as well as active decisions to make sells along the way. Consequently, this metric provides a fuzzy indicator of buying prowess under the best of circumstances. Importantly, a fund can exhibit a substantial positive return from stock selection even when the buy skill is moderate or negative. The weak relationship between return from stock selection and buying ability is illustrated in the following example.

Consider an equity fund that holds approximately forty positions. Each quarter, on average, three new stocks are purchased for the fund, and each is given a portfolio weight of one-half its benchmark weight (the initial weight). Typically, this fund keeps only one of the quarterly buys (the keepers) for several years while selling the other two within a few months of their initial purchase, having determined they were poor choices. Once a holding is determined to be a keeper, it is given an active weight (i.e., above benchmark weight). Only three out of four of the keepers eventually go on to outperform (become "winners"). These numbers indicate that the fund's rate of success at identifying strong stocks is approximately 25%, or three out of twelve (number of winners per year/number of buys per year). Over a twelve-month period, the fund buys twelve stocks, realizes eight are mistakes and sells them relatively quickly, and of the four that remain in the fund, three go on to outperform. Not what might immediately come to mind as highly effective buying, but it can get the job done. It's possible because the fund maintains small weights across all new buys, then substantially increases the size of the keepers within six months of their purchase, and then makes subsequent adds to the proven winners. This results in most of the fund's capital being invested in stocks that outperform (winners) or that at least match the benchmark returns (other keepers). Conventional analytics very likely would show that this fund both delivers alpha (outperforms its benchmark) and generates a positive return from stock selection. And it is doing this with a modest success rate in purchasing winning stocks.

This example is emblematic of the limitations of conventional analytics. The strong fund level returns and the positive return from stock selection are real and accurate. They might also be misconstrued as suggesting strong buying. The reality is very different. This fund purchases alpha generating stocks only once in every four tries. This modest success rate is compensated for by quickly selling ineffective buys and a successful sizing regime. Rather than buying skill, it is the fund's skilled selling and skilled sizing that are delivering strong results. Skill confusion like this heavily burdens the fund assessment process.

Batting Average and Slugging Ratio
The batting average and slugging ratio are basic metrics expressing relative success in position ownership. The batting average can be calculated using two methods: One involves the number of outperforming periods over time, and the other is based on the number of positions owned with positive returns. The most frequently used method involves periods. For this approach, the basic measure is the number of periods when the fund outperformed its benchmark divided by the total number of periods observed. The most common time interval used is monthly, although daily, weekly,

and quarterly periodicity can be used. The result indicates the percent or rate of time that the fund outperformed (i.e., the batting average is the number of outperforming months divided by total months considered).

The alternative or position count approach is calculated as the number of positions held in the fund that generated realized and unrealized gains (winners) divided by the total number of positions held in the fund over a specific time interval (e.g., twelve months). The result indicates the fraction or rate of positions held that generated a positive return. Both approaches measure a form of fund success (based on winning periods or winning positions). Neither form of batting average includes information about the level of returns generated by the winners, nor does it factor in the weights of the winners (i.e., how significantly they contributed to fund success).

References to this metric usually suggest that—all other things being equal—it's better for a fund to have a higher batting average. In the real world, however, pare-wise comparisons among funds are rarely that simple. For example, a fund with a relatively low batting average can regularly outperform a similar second fund with a higher batting average. This seeming paradox of batting average and results can occur when (1) the first fund buys winners that are more vibrant (higher average price increases) than those purchased by the second fund; and (2) the first fund gives its winners higher portfolio weights and achieves this more quickly as compared to the second fund. In essence, the first fund is capturing more fund lift from a lower batting average by concentrating a greater portion of its capital in the strongest positions. The question then is: What insight may be drawn from batting average? It's not clear. Yet batting average is routinely consulted during the fund assessment process.

The slugging ratio provides more information about the fund's average winner and loser than does the batting average. That's because the slugging ratio includes both the frequency of winners and losers and a measure of the magnitude of return generated by the fund's average winner and loser. The slugging ratio is computed as the average gain from the fund's winners divided by the absolute value of the average loss from its losers. The gains and losses reflect a good bit of information about positions, including the frequency of winners and losers, the average duration of each, the average magnitude of gain and loss across all holdings, and the capital invested in winning and losing positions. Slugging ratio, therefore, compares the average profit and loss generated by the fund's successful and unsuccessful positions. Ratios greater than 1.0 indicate that the fund earns more from its average winner than it gives back on its average loser, and vice versa. Of course, ratios higher than 1.0 might be due to any combination of manager skills, including a goodly number of winners (strong buying skill), winners being built up in weight relatively quickly while limiting the capital invested in losers (effective sizing skill), or winners and losers being harvested effectively (productive selling skill). Generally speaking, the higher the slugging ratio, the better, since by definition when the profit from all winners is greater than the losses from all losers, the result is a positive return for the fund. Although the slugging ratio provides a bit more information than the batting average, it falls well short of indicating exactly which of the manager's decisions or skills were most responsible for the fund's results.

Considering Multiple Metrics Together

Combining the batting average and slugging ratio with a fund's excess returns provides greater insight than any of these measures alone. Consider a fund that is beating its benchmark and whose positions depict a high slugging ratio (say, 1.4). If this fund also had a batting average of 56%, it suggests that on average, many positions are contributing to the fund's overall success. Alternatively, if this same fund's batting average were 25%, it would point to a relatively small number of positions generating substantial gains and, more than likely, that losers are being managed effectively so as to limit their drag on fund results. These are precisely the types of helpful inferences that can be drawn by batting average and slugging ratio. Such impressions might then be further explored with the help of additional conventional analytics, such as attribution, upside/downside capture, information ratio, and active share. The quality of the fund could be further pursued through manager interviews and spot-checking a handful of winning and losing positions. That's pretty much how the typical fund analysis unfolds. At the conclusion, however, there is still a meaningful gap between what can be surmised and what skills are actually driving fund results.

Sharpe Ratio and Information Ratio

These ratios each provide a risk-adjusted measure of a fund's excess returns. These metrics accommodate comparisons across funds with regard to how much excess return is being generated per unit of riskiness undertaken.[5] Each ratio is computed as the mean of a fund's excess returns over time divided by the standard deviation of the excess returns. The Sharpe Ratio computes excess return as the difference between the fund's returns and a risk-free return (typically a short-term US Treasury), whereas the Information Ratio computes excess return as the difference between the returns of the fund and its benchmark. For both measures, higher positive ratios are better in that they indicate more excess returns are being generated per unit of risk. In contrast, ratios less than 1.0 reflect relatively high levels of volatility (riskiness) per unit of return generated. Negative ratios confirm overall weak performance due to a negative relative return.

Skilled managers are thought to be those whose fund returns support ratios greater than 1.0. Assuming that is the case, exactly what skills are responsible for the attractive ratio? Is it strong buying? Perhaps effective selling? Or maybe astute sizing? Possibly even well-implemented risk management? As with other conventional analytics, these ratios are helpful in understanding how a fund performed but support only inferences about skills. Consequently, their value in helping to gauge the likelihood that a fund might outperform going forward seems modest.

Active Share

Active share is a measure of how much a fund's positions differ from its benchmark. It's calculated by adding up the difference between each stock's weight in the fund and its benchmark weight, and then dividing by two. Greater differences result in higher active share. Martijn Cremers and Antti Petajisto, who conceived of this metric, initially suggested that high active share was an indicator of skill and likely future outperformance.[6] Cremers later backed away from these assertions in a subsequent paper.[7]

What's clear is that high active share can amplify the impact of skilled (or unskilled) investing. Its effect is similar to that of leverage or gearing. Overweighting a fund's strongest performing holdings will drive up returns. Conversely, heavy allocations to a fund's underperforming positions will lower returns. As Cremers himself concluded, high active share benefits those managers who are skilled at both identifying strong stocks and sizing them effectively. There is scant evidence, however, that active share in and of itself can help identify skill. The disconnect between levels of active share and alpha has not, thus far, diminished its prevalence on fund search checklists or among manager interview questions. High active share and high concentration (low position count) continue to be searched out in hopes that when these construction characteristics are present, there might also be a skilled manager in residence who can capitalize on these features to deliver excess returns.

Further Thoughts on Skill

In addition to the conventional analytics currently used by investment practitioners, there are a number of extensions of this type of analysis discussed in the financial literature. A few of these somewhat novel analytics are described in this section.

Multifactor Alpha

Many academic papers assess manager skill using a multifactor regression of a fund's total returns. The most common method for computing multifactor alpha is the so-called Fama French plus Carhart or four-factor model.[8] The four factors used in this regression are (1) beta or the market itself, (2) the relative performance of large cap stocks to small cap stocks, (3) the relative performance of growth stocks to value stocks, and (4) the relative performance of high momentum stocks to low momentum stocks. Academic studies mostly focus on identifying how many funds, from among a large number of funds examined, actually provide a positive four-factor alpha. The majority of these studies conclude that equity managers by and large demonstrate no discernible skill, meaning that after accounting for fees the majority of funds analyzed deliver alphas that are zero or negative. This conclusion is consistent with Sharpe's arithmetic discussed in chapter 2. A further criticism of active management found in this type of research is that even where the residual alphas are positive, such residuals tend not to be consistent over time. Up for debate is whether this type of analysis actually demonstrates the presence or absence of skill. Or perhaps its purpose really is to help explain the market dynamics under which the fund did or did not generate excess returns. Multifactor alphas are used within the fund assessment process today, but not as universally as other conventional analytics.

Fund Size

Researchers Berk and Green suggest that skill can be inferred from fund size.[9] Their thesis is that skilled managers will initially generate sufficient excess returns so as to attract inflows (i.e., investor capital). Then, assuming that markets are efficient and that investors act rationally (i.e., make choices to maximize expected wealth), Berk and Green further suggest that the inflows will continue until the fund is larger than can be accommodated effectively by the manager's best stock ideas. They hypothesize that fund capital in excess of the manager's best ideas might then be invested in lesser stocks and/or indexed. According to this model the fund ultimately grows its assets to the point where it generates a level of excess returns sufficient only to cover fees with no excess returns left for the investors. As Berk and Green state: "In other words, the flow–performance relationship makes the persistence in net alphas disappear." It is an intriguing concept, especially for those inclined to view the world through the lens of the efficient market hypothesis. If true, this theory lends credence to the notion that superior returns are more likely from smaller funds. And larger funds tend to exhaust all available skill just to break even. If correct, this idea may help point capital allocators toward that portion of the pond where alpha is likely to be found (i.e., funds with small to modest assets under management relative to their investable universes). This fund size strategy could help reduce the scope of search undertaken for a fund. It's unclear whether it will actually help uncover skilled funds.

Fund Covariance

Another attempt at skill identification concerns identifying funds that outperform, and that also hold the same or similar positions as other outperforming funds. Cohen, Coval, and Pastor observed that high-performing funds that also reflect a high Jensen's alpha (risk-adjusted returns) tend to hold the same alpha generating stocks as other high-performing funds.[10] Their research suggests that across peer funds (i.e., similar style, strategy, and construction) that generated alpha, those that owned the same outperforming stocks are likely to possess skill. Whereas funds from the same peer groups whose alpha was based on different outperforming stocks benefited more from luck. This is an intriguing approach to fund analysis, yet it provides no understanding of which skills generated the desired alpha.

Observations

Efforts within academia continue to identify attributes that further explain the sources of a fund's excess returns, or lack thereof. Much like conventional analytics now in wide use, these concepts do not directly identify or measure skill. And while all inquiries into what makes an equity fund tick are welcome, the need for robust measures of skill and its persistence are now needed.

Conclusion

Actively managed equities offer the potential for capturing excess returns. Selecting which funds to invest in, however, is not easy. Fund assessment today is significantly hampered by the reliance on conventional analytics. While these analytics provide much-needed insights into a fund's returns, construction, and riskiness, their utility does not extend into the identification of skill.

The shortcomings of conventional analytics in ferreting out skill lie in the data used in their calculation. For the most part, these analytics rely upon a fund's return time series or its history of daily holdings. These data well support the computation of numerous metrics explaining the sources of past results. They can, however, deliver only weak insights into manager skills. Capital allocators, therefore, must infer the presence or absence of skill based on these metrics. This intuiting is error-prone and frequently leads to incorrect conclusions.

Skill assessment, it is argued, requires new thinking. And this starts with an updated definition of skill, one where skill reflects the combined effects of professional judgment and investment processes. These two qualities are well within the manager's control. Moreover, the relative consistency of these qualities appears useful in assessing a fund's likelihood in generating excess returns going forward.

The examination of several commonly used conventional analytics underscores how their results can be easily misinterpreted. Inferences about manager skill drawn from these analytics are at best questionable and frequently just plain wrong. The need for newer analytics is clear. Descriptions of several newer analytics that enable capital allocators to more directly probe manager skill are presented in the following chapters.

4   Information Advantage

Having knowledge but lacking the power to express it clearly is no better than never having any ideas at all.
—Pericles

A manager's ability to regularly buy stocks that outperform is commonly referred to as their information advantage. It is thought to reflect the ability to identify investment opportunities well before they are priced into the market. This concept underlies the search for skilled managers and equity fund allocations. Absent is a generally agreed-upon description of this manager quality. Also lacking are methods for detecting the existence of an information advantage and its measurement. In addressing these deficits this chapter provides an intuitive definition for the information advantage and describes one method for its computation.

The Information Advantage

Regularly identifying successful buying opportunities ahead of the crowd is a great skill. Known as a manager's information advantage, this ability includes both sourcing potential new buys with alpha generating capacity and completing such analyses in time to capitalize on their anticipated price movements. The benefits of a strong information advantage are clear: The chances of generating fund-level alpha go up as the number and quality of successful new buys increases. Whereas when the manager's typical new buys are weak or barely outperforming their benchmark, it is much more difficult to generate fund-level alpha (as discussed in chapter 2). To be useful, the information advantage should support understanding the quality of a fund's buys, meaning their average relative strength and the profile of their return generation over time.

Analytics consistent with this description go a long way toward answering a range of important questions, such as:

- What is the magnitude of the information advantage?
- How long after the initial purchase do the prices of new buys begin to take off?
- Are strong buys being sized effectively?
- How long does the information advantage last?
- How consistent is the information advantage over time and across sectors?

Answers to questions like these can deliver insight into the quality of the stock purchases that are generating fund results. And it is the impact of these purchases, repeated again and again, that define the fund's information advantage.

Calculating the Information Advantage

Initial insight into the information advantage can be computed using a variation on the well-established contribution to total return analysis. The key modification is that the fund's results are presented over a series of time intervals. They express the relative contribution from new buys over time—soon after purchase up to the fund's longest holding period. Before describing how the information advantage is computed, it is worth quickly reviewing the basic method for calculating contribution.

The Basics

Contribution analysis describes the impact that each individual holding (or groups of holdings) had in generating a fund's total returns. For a single holding, its one-day contribution is computed as:

$$bCS_{ji} = (SR_{ji})(SW_{ji})$$

where:

C refers to the contribution amount as a percentage (fraction of the total return)

S refers to a single holding or stock

CS_{ji} = the contribution from an individual holding (j) on the day of analysis (i)

SR_{ji} = the return of holding (j) on day (i)

SW_{ji} = the portfolio weight of the holding (j) on day (i)

Consider this simple example. For a particular day, a fund holds two positions, A and B. At the beginning of the day each position has a fund weight of 50%. During the same day position A earned a 10% return and B earned a −5% return. The contribution from A to the fund's total return is computed as $(0.50) \times (0.10) = 0.05$, or 5.0%. Similarly, the contribution of B on the same day is computed as $(0.50) \times (-0.05) = -0.025$, or −2.5%. The fund's total return equals the sum of the contribution values for holdings A and B, which in this example is $0.50 + -0.025$, which equals 0.25 or 2.5%.

As can be observed, basic contribution analysis provides a clear measure of how each holding added to or detracted from the fund's total return. Computing results for subgroups (e.g., sectors, global regions, factors) is performed similarly where the combined weights and weighted returns for subgroups replace the information for individual holdings. Contribution measures involving longer time periods (e.g., weeks, months, years) are computed as the time-weighted return of the daily linked values.[1]

Contribution by Age
The information advantage is a form of contribution analysis, as mentioned. What distinguishes it from other contribution analyses is the concept of position age. Rather than grouping positions by sector, global region, factor, or other common characteristics, the computation of the information advantage groups positions by age cohorts. The method used in computing the information advantage is as follows:

Step 1. On each day in the analysis time period, the age of each position (number of days held) is determined. Ages can range from one day up to many years.

Step 2. For each day of the analysis time period, the fund's positions are sorted into five quintiles based on age such that the first quintile contains the youngest 20% of positions by count, the second quintile contains the second youngest 20% of positions, and so on. It's common for each quintile to reflect a range of ages and for some ranges to be longer or shorter than others. Since the fund's number of positions may not be evenly divisible by five, the quintile position counts may not be equal.

Step 3. The daily contribution for each age quintile is then computed. It's calculated as the sum of the individual contribution values for all holdings, on each day, within each quintile.

Step 4. Total annual contribution values for each quintile are then computed. This is accomplished by linking the daily contribution values within each quintile and annualizing the final results as appropriate. Positions held for a relatively short time may impact the contribution values for only the first and second quintiles. Whereas positions held longer may impact the contribution results for up to three, four, or even five quintiles (i.e., a holding will move from one quintile to the next as its age in the fund increases over the analysis timeframe).

Step 5. The total contribution values for each quintile are then compared to the fund's return to compute the relative contribution of each quintile. The results of this age-based contribution analysis are then plotted so that the information advantage can be visualized. A basic plot of the information advantage includes the relative contribution values and the age ranges.

Interpretation of the information advantage can be aided with some additional explanation of the underlying analytics.

First up is the concept of *relative contribution*. This term denotes that the contribution values for each of the five quintiles are expressed relative to the fund's total return. Hence, a positive relative contribution indicates that the quintile outperformed the fund's return. A negative relative contribution shows that the quintile underperformed the fund's return. The return values, therefore, inform us as to whether a particular age quintile contributed positively or negatively to the fund's total return and by how much.

The second item concerns the average age for quintiles being expressed as a range. This is due primarily to (i) changing position counts over time, which can result in shortening or elongating the age intervals held in each quintile, and (ii) changes in the fund's turnover rate, which can alter the overall time horizon the average position is held. Consequently, the distribution of ages on day one of the analysis may be vastly smaller or larger than on other days. Thus, the range indicates both the position ages accounted for in each quintile and the variability of the daily age distribution over time.

A third consideration is that position age can be computed as the date between initial purchase and any future day (calendar age) or the weighted average of the time that each capital addition is executed. Regarding the latter, a position initiated on January 1 with a 2% weight and then given a 2% add on July 1 of the same year would, on December 31, have an average age of nine months (2% for twelve months and 2% for six months). The weighted age is used in this chapter and throughout the examples presented in this book.

The fourth and final point is that a fund's information advantage can morph from year to year. For example, a fund's information advantage may be shorter over the most recent three years as compared to the three years prior. Or the fund's information advantage may now be very front-loaded (i.e., strongest in the first two quintiles) whereas it was more back-loaded in the past. Examining what, if anything, has changed in the length and/or dynamism of the information advantage over time offers obvious benefits. Several examples illustrating the value of computing this form of information advantage are presented next.

Visualizing the Information Advantage

Individuals learn in a variety of ways. For a great many people, visualizations of analytic results make them more impactful—thereby supporting clearer interpretation and more rapid absorption of critical information. This section presents the results of five information advantage analyses as visualizations or plots. This group of examples demonstrates the utility of this analysis over a range of fund success levels.

Figure 4.1 depicts the information advantage of a global real estate investment trust (REIT) fund over a three-year time period (2021–2023). This was a challenging three-year period for the global REIT industry (the REIT market was down nearly 30% in 2022). Nevertheless, this fund did well, having beaten its benchmark by roughly 2% over this three-year period. The first notable item in figure 4.1 is that most of the fund's positions have an age of less than twenty-four months and that positions in the fifth quintile have ages ranging from twenty-five months to over thirteen years (long tail). Attention is then drawn to the fund's relative contribution by age, which is close to zero for the first three quintiles, then moves up to 25 basis points (bps) in the fourth quintile and then down to −34 bps in the

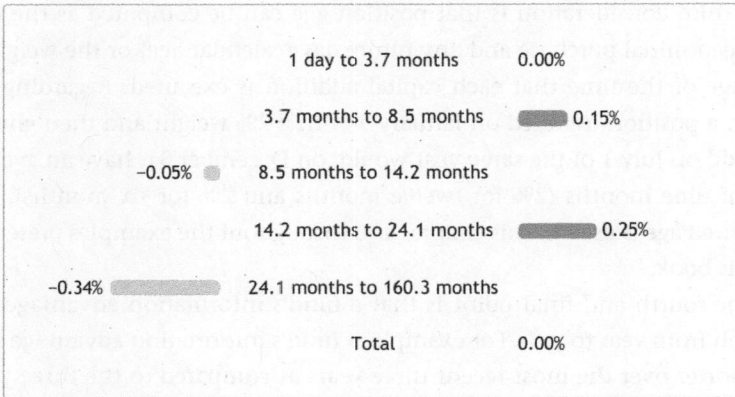

	1 day to 3.7 months	0.00%
	3.7 months to 8.5 months	0.15%
−0.05%	8.5 months to 14.2 months	
	14.2 months to 24.1 months	0.25%
−0.34%	24.1 months to 160.3 months	
	Total	0.00%

Figure 4.1
Steady beginnings and a modest finish.

fifth quintile (the black bars indicate positive relative contribution and the gray bars indicate negative relative contribution). This dynamic means that positions generally perform consistently over all five quintiles. This profile suggests that the fund's information advantage is roughly two years and that positions tend to be managed effectively as they age.

Takeaways.   What has been learned from this single analysis? It appears that the fund's information advantage lasts about twenty-four months and that there is no significant change in relative contribution during this period. The results hint at the likelihood that this fund is effective at harvesting positions—trimming and selling those that are losing their steam while holding on to positions that continue to contribute well.

Figure 4.2 depicts the information advantage of a value fund. This fund was battling a headwind for the four years shown (2021–2024). It underperformed its benchmark by roughly −3% annually over this period. What catches the eye immediately is the negative relative contribution from the first quintile (ages under three months) of −1.01%. Over the subsequent twelve months (quintiles two and three) contribution is roughly zero. Then between fifteen and twenty-four months the relative contribution goes to 1.02%. The final quintile holds some positions up to six years and provides a relative contribution of 0.13%.

The negative to flat relative contribution during the initial three quintiles (day one to fifteen months) suggest this value fund is getting into positions

−1.01%	1 day to 4.3 months	
−0.05%	4.3 months to 9.6 months	
−0.10%	9.6 months to 15.2 months	
	15.2 months to 23.3 months	1.02%
	23.3 months to 71.1 months	0.13%
	Total	0.00%

Figure 4.2
The challenges of value investing.

a bit early. If this is the case, then it may prove prudent for the fund to initiate positions with a modest fund weight and then build them up quickly as they begin to prove their theses. The usefulness of this sizing approach can be explored further by assessing the information advantage over multiple consecutive time periods in order to confirm its consistency. This investigation can be supported with the help of returns, relative returns, and other conventional metrics for the same intervals.

Takeaways.   The fund's poor overall relative return is not fully explained by this analysis. What can be observed is that the fund tends to get into positions a bit early. Having too much capital invested in positions before they begin to hit their stride may be one of the causes of weak results. A fuller understanding of what is causing this fund's underperformance and the likelihood of a turnaround can be aided with a look at the buying, selling, and sizing skills described in the next chapter.

The information advantage for a global growth fund is presented in figure 4.3. This is a highly successful fund that has generated a relative return of over 5%. The plot shows that in the first quintile the relative contribution is 1.22% followed by 1.48% in the second quintile. This relatively high contribution is occurring within 3.5 months of purchasing new stocks. The relative contribution essentially goes to zero for the third and fourth quintiles. Then in the fifth quintile the relative contribution drops to −2.31% for positions held longer than eleven months.

	1 day to 1.7 months	1.22%
	1.7 months to 3.5 months	1.48%
−0.35%	3.5 months to 6.0 months	
−0.03%	6.0 months to 10.9 months	
−2.31%	10.9 months to 24.2 months	
	Total	0.00%

Figure 4.3
Information duration and turnover.

This fund's information advantage is clearly front-loaded. Capturing the potential of this dynamic requires getting to full position size very quickly. Given the somewhat abrupt drop-off in relative contribution after one year, it's easy to see why this fund might benefit from a higher turnover rate than many of its peers.[2]

Takeaways. The fund appears to be sufficiently aware of its information advantage. This is suggested by the high relative contributions for the initial two quintiles, reflecting both strong returns and meaningful position sizes. The relative contribution falls off noticeably for positions held more than one year. It's reasonable to speculate that this fund possesses a strong buying skill, which can be confirmed using other newer analytics. The selling skill may be challenged in that it appears some positions are being held well beyond their productive lives. It's difficult to infer much about the sizing skill from this analysis. An analysis of the basic skills would provide useful insights now missing regarding which skills are driving the results.

Observing if and how the information advantage changes from one time period to the next can provide preliminary insight into the consistency of skills and processes. The fund depicted in this example is successful, having generated 1.50% of relative return over a ten-year span. The fund's information advantage for two consecutive five-year periods is presented in figures 4.4a and 4.4b. The relative contribution by age varies considerably for quintiles 1 through 4, as can be observed in the two figures. From the initial

(a)

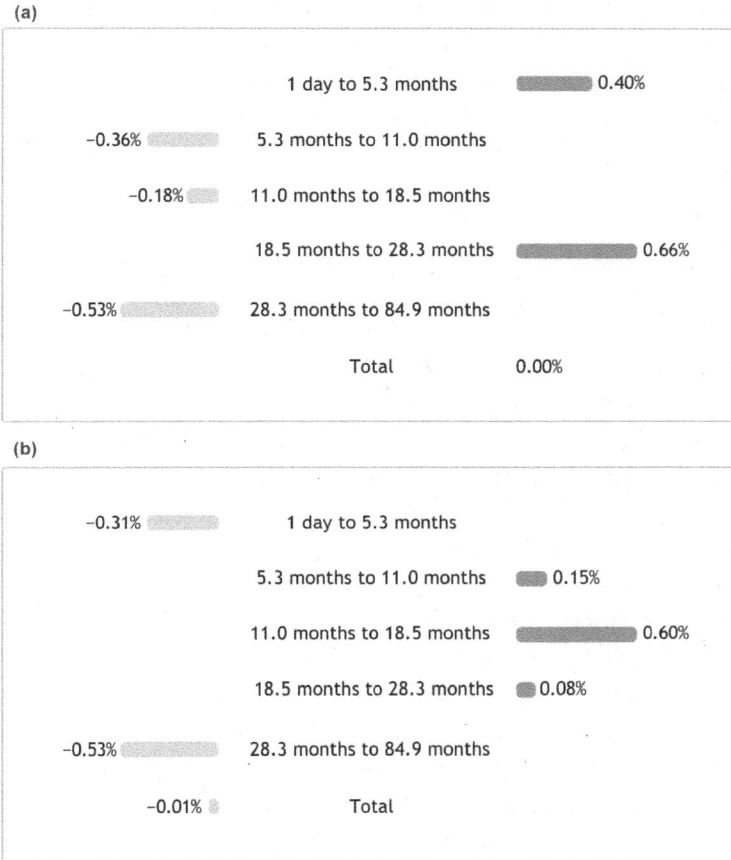

	1 day to 5.3 months	0.40%
−0.36%	5.3 months to 11.0 months	
−0.18%	11.0 months to 18.5 months	
	18.5 months to 28.3 months	0.66%
−0.53%	28.3 months to 84.9 months	
	Total	0.00%

(b)

−0.31%	1 day to 5.3 months	
	5.3 months to 11.0 months	0.15%
	11.0 months to 18.5 months	0.60%
	18.5 months to 28.3 months	0.08%
−0.53%	28.3 months to 84.9 months	
−0.01%	Total	

Figure 4.4
Shifting contributions.

period to the second period the results changed as follows: Values for the first quintile declined by −1.71%, values for the second quintile improved by 0.51%, values for the third quintile improved by 0.78%, and values for the fourth quintile declined by −0.58%. There is no change in the fifth quintile. Most notable is the drop in contribution from the youngest positions. This may be due to getting into positions a bit earlier. This possibility is supported by the uptick in contribution levels for the second and third quintiles, beginning five months after purchase.

Takeaways. Consistency with regard to success is a valued quality. The information advantage for this fund varies across the two consecutive five-year periods studied. These results lead to the inference that the funds may still be buying effectively while getting into new stocks sooner than before. The analysis of basic skills plus conventional analytics can be used to determine the correctness of this inference.

Conclusion

Possessing knowledge ahead of the crowd enables funds to take investment actions that can generate excess returns. This ability with regard to purchasing stocks is referred to as an information advantage. Fund outperformance together with a clear and consistent information advantage provides a useful addition to fund screening metrics.

The well-known contribution analysis analytic is used to investigate the information advantage. The key extension being that position age is used as the independent variable rather than more conventional groupings, such as sector, size, and financial factor. Age-based contribution provides a look at how a fund's new buys contribute to total return over their holding periods.

The information advantage results also provide some insight into fund skills. This includes inferring which skill may be driving results (i.e., buying, selling, sizing) and its consistency. The duration of the information advantage can also help assess if a fund's turnover rate is in line with the alpha generating capacity of its holdings.

The information advantage is discussed first among the newer analytics for two reasons: First, its results are high-level and more inferential rather than direct measures of skill—a clear yet modest advancement over previous analytics. Second, it demonstrates how, with some basic rethinking of what skill means and how it can be assessed, it is possible to better understand the knowledge and ability of equity fund managers. The information advantage considered examines the relative contribution from positions as they age. Future innovations may provide different and even clearer insights into a fund's buying advantage.

5   Skill Is Where the Action Is

Action is the foundational key to all success.
—Pablo Picasso

Manager skill is extensively researched and poorly understood. One reason for this paradox is the prevailing methods used in investigating skill. For the most part, traditional analytics attempt to assess skill using fund outcomes, that is, the fund's return series and its daily holdings (as discussed in chapter 3). These outcome data do not lend themselves to meaningful measures of skill. They support the inference of skill. And such inferences can be helpful when they happen to be in line with actual skill. Unfortunately, these inferences can also be incorrect and misleading. Knowing when an inference is accurate or inaccurate is close to impossible. And therein lies the dilemma. The shortcomings of conventional analytics can be mitigated, in good part, with the addition of analytics that are orthogonal to conventional techniques. These newer analytics assess skills based on the decisions that change fund composition and therefore drive subsequent results. Decisions that regularly contribute to future outperformance are positive skills. Those that regularly undermine future outperformance are negative skills. When combined with traditional analytics, these newer (decision-based) analytics provide rigorous insights into which skills are driving fund success and which are thwarting it.

The Anatomy of a Decision

A number of approaches can be used to identify manager decisions. Three of the most popular approaches involve looking at individual trade data, analyzing what is referred to as a position episode, and implementing methods based on manager actions. Each approach offers distinct pluses and minuses, as will be discussed.

Trade Data

Trade data refers to the analysis of each and every trade involving the purchase or sale of stocks. The benefits of trade data include its ready availability, tremendous granularity, and strongly intuitive appeal. The availability stems from the extensive infrastructure used to capture trade data. This data is used to confirm the completion of orders (what's been purchased or sold) and to instantiate accounting transactions, which ultimately drives numerous downstream analytics like fund performance measurement, attribution analysis, and a host of risk analyses. The granularity is self-evident—it includes each lot of stocks traded, the amount, the price, and the date. It is easy to appreciate the intuitive appeal of trade data as representing decisions. When stocks are purchased to initiate a new position, that certainly seems like a decision. Similarly, when more stocks are purchased for an existing position or when shares in an existing position are sold, these seem like decisions as well. There is, however, more to a series of trades than just manager decisions. There are liquidity constraints and fund flows, which can make individual trades less informative than presumed.

Liquidity constraints can result in a single decision to make a stock purchase being executed through numerous trades. For example, the manager may send an order to the internal trading desk to start purchasing 100,000 shares of company XYZ. The accumulation of all 100,000 shares may be accomplished in a day or two for liquid stocks with just a handful or so of trades, or it might take a number of weeks to complete requiring scores of individual trades for relatively illiquid stocks. Which means that for the most part there is a one-to-many relationship between a manager's decision and the number of trades needed to effect the decision. Just how many trades will be required and how many days they'll occur over depends upon the number of shares needed, the float of the stock, the liquidity of those shares, and the manager's tolerance for market impact. And this one-to-many relationship holds for all types of manager decision, such as initiating a new position, adding to or trimming an existing position, and exiting a position.

Further complicating the use of trade data are inflows and outflows. Fund flows often generate so-called involuntary trades. Inflows usually need to be invested, and this requires buys or adds. If the inflows are invested pro rata across all of the fund's existing positions, this results in lots of stock buying with little to no change in the weights of the fund's positions. The reverse is true for outflows—lots of sells but essentially no changes to position weights. Consequently, it is debatable whether trades due to flows that are executed pro rata should or should not be used to assess skill. Proponents of including such trades suggest that leaving all position weights as they were is in itself a decision. The opposition view is that if the weights don't change, the net effect is no decision. There is no disagreement that if the inflows are allocated on a non–pro rata basis the fund is clearly changing its bets, and that decisions are definitely being made and implemented. It is to a large extent possible to separate intentional trading (decisions) from involuntary trades (nondecisions) if they are appropriately tagged or identified as they are being executed. This accounting of the reasons for individual trades is rarely done, however. The upshot is that trade data can provide fuzzy information about decisions when liquidity constraints are significant and/or when the level of fund flows are frequent or substantial.

Critical assumptions are required to analyze trade data as well. Consider buying prowess. In order to compute the effectiveness of a buy trade, there needs to be a time horizon over which the returns of new buys are assessed. This could be a few days, several weeks, or a number of months. Determining which period to use is obviously important. Using a period that is too short can miss alpha generation that is somewhat back-ended. Picking a horizon that is too long can drag down the results, as many stocks will have stopped generating alpha and have become either dead money or started to round trip. Testing several time horizons can help choose the most appropriate analysis period. Referencing the fund's information advantage can help with this task.

Takeaways. Skill analysis based on trade data can produce insightful results. Understanding how liquidity and fund flows are being addressed within these analyses helps in interpreting their results.

Episodes
A hybrid use of trade data involves what are termed position episodes. For any individual stock, an episode consists of the time between when a position commences and it is fully liquidated (i.e., from the moment it has a nonzero weight until it once again has a zero weight). Position episodes

include all of the trades related to a position throughout a single ownership episode. This would include the initial buy, all subsequent adds and trims, and the final liquidation. The analysis can be based on individual trades or daily net trades.

Episode analysis offers the same data benefits described above. The fact that each episode has its own unique start date and end date means that this form of skill analysis does not require the same number of assumptions as does analyzing trade data alone. Each individual episode contains the full complement of decisions made by the manager with respect to the position involved. Included among these decisions are the initial buy, each subsequent add, all partial sells or trims, and the final sell or liquidation. The profitability of each episode can be computed using its trade data, market returns, and corporate actions. The profitability of episodes thus becomes a measure of manager skill. Episodes that generate a profit or net gain indicate success. This means that, over the episode, the impacts from skilled decisions outweighed the impacts from unproductive or unskilled decisions. Alternatively, episodes with a net loss indicate that the impacts from unskilled decisions outweighed the impacts from skilled decisions. Computing the profitability of the entire episode circumvents the need to evaluate each trade uniquely.

Episodes and their components can be summed and averaged to indicate broad skill levels. For example, the number of profitable episodes divided by the number of total episodes offers an alternative approach to computing batting average. Similarly, the ratio of the average gain from positive episodes divided by the average loss from negative episodes provides an interesting approach to computing a slugging ratio. The net gain (or loss) across all episodes can be computed, and this value can be thought of as indicative of the manager's buy skill. Additionally, episodes can be plotted so that all of the decisions contained may be visualized. These visualizations can include contextual information such as stock price, stock returns, price volatility, benchmark returns, etc. Such visualizations can help in understanding how and when a manager makes their best decisions (i.e., acts most skillfully). Plotting a group of episodes as overlapping images allows for the visual assessment of decision consistency and other patterns. Because each episode is inclusive of all trades for that position start to end, it also reflects the effects of fund flows. Repeated ownership of the same stock would constitute multiple episodes. If a stock is initially purchased (its fund weight becomes nonzero) and then is fully liquidated (fund weight back to zero), these two events bookmark the beginning and ending of an episode. If this same stock were repurchased (a nonzero fund weight reestablished) sometime later, this would denote the beginning of a new, or in this case second, episode.

Takeaways. Episode analysis builds directly upon trade data. Computing episode profitability can be done without the use of the many assumptions needed when working with trade data alone. Episode analysis provides interesting insights into skills and affords the flexibility needed to support a number of granular investigations.

Actions

An action is defined as the change in a position's weight, from one day to the next, that cannot be accounted for by price movements alone. It's computed as the difference between (i) a position's actual weight at the end of a market day and (ii) its expected weight or no-action weight for the same day. The no-action weight for a position describes its expected weight at the end of a day if no actions had been taken since the end of the prior day. The no-action weight may be higher, lower, or the same as its weight at the end of the day prior depending upon the position's one-day return relative to the one-day return of all other positions in the fund. A nonzero difference between the actual weight and the no-action weight means that intentional changes were made to one or more positions. In other words, the construction or bets within the fund were reconfigured. This relatively simple calculation provides unambiguous insight into when decisions take place, the types of decisions occurring, and the magnitude of such decisions. Among their benefits is that actions are conceptually straightforward. Moreover, they are computed using readily available daily holdings data. Data of this type is maintained in accounting systems and other databases supporting the analyses of performance, attribution, and risk.

Actions allow for the direct quantification of distinct skills, such as buying, sizing, and selling. This is done with the use of counterfactual portfolios (discussed in chapter 6). In addition to facilitating both rigorous and granular assessment of skills, actions also accommodate fund flows thoughtfully. Consider the following: If a fund receives an inflow and that capital is allocated to all existing positions on a pro rata basis, then from an action perspective nothing happened. The actual weights of all positions would be equal to their expected or no-action weights. If, on the other hand, an inflow is allocated in a manner other than pro rata, then a series of actions would have occurred. Specifically, positions whose actual weight is greater than their no-action weight would have received an add. Positions whose actual weight is less than their no-action weight would have experienced a trim. This simple algebra enables actions to work equally well with relatively low-flow institutional accounts as well as publicly traded mutual funds and electronically traded funds.

Takeaways. Actions provide clear indications of manager decisions. They do this by reflecting intentional changes in a position's weight. Actions also accommodate fund flows effectively. They do this by indicating when flows are simply added to existing positions versus used to alter the bets in the fund. Actions are used within the construction of counterfactual portfolios that quantify manager skills broadly and with high levels of granularity.

Summary
Each of the methods for identifying manager decisions described above supports computing measures of skill. The rigor, discreteness, and granularity of skill measures possible does vary across the approaches. Since there is no industry standard for identifying manager decisions at this time, capital allocators may wish to assess skill using more than one of these methods.

Throughout the remainder of this book, however, skill investigations are conducted using actions evaluated within counterfactual portfolios.[1] The reason for choosing this approach is entirely pragmatic. The author was granted extraordinary access to analytic software based on actions and counterfactual portfolios by one of the leading software and data providers. This opportunity was simply too good to pass up. Importantly, it enables all of the examples presented throughout the balance of this book to demonstrate what types of insights are generally available from the newer analytics. Skill and investment process results based on trade data and position episodes are of comparable informational quality. Prior to shifting attention to the computation of skills, it seems appropriate to review in more detail how actions are calculated.

Calculating Actions

Once again, an action is when the weight of a position changes from one day to the next and such change cannot be explained by price movement alone. The basic method for computing an action is as follows:

$$\text{Action}_{i,t} = \text{AWT}_{i,t} - \text{NAWT}_{i,t}$$

where:

$\text{Action}_{i,t}$ = the action computed for position$_i$ at the end of day$_t$

$\text{AWT}_{i,t}$ = the actual weight of position$_i$ at the end of day$_t$

$\text{NAWT}_{i,t}$ = the no action weight of position$_i$ at the end of day$_t$

i = an individual position or stock within the fund

t = the day on which the action is being computed

Positive differences indicate a new buy (when $\text{NAWT}_{i,t-1}=0$); otherwise it indicates an add to an existing position. Negative differences indicate a liquidation of an existing position (when $\text{AWT}_{i,t}=0$); otherwise it indicates a trim of an existing position. The larger the differences, the more significant the action. Differences of zero or near zero indicate no action. Actions calculated in this manner are affected by flows only when flows are applied other than pro rata. Intra-day trades are captured as elements of end-of-day position weights. Decisions that take multiple days to implement can be condensed analytically into single actions, as described in the next section. First it is worth reviewing two basic examples of how actions are computed.

A two-day history for a long-only equity fund is presented in table 5.1. The fund holds three positions: A, B, and C with weights of 20%, 30%, and 50%, respectively, as of the end of day$_{t-1}$. Given the daily price movements on day$_t$, the no-action weights for the positions at the end of that day are computed as 25% for A, 32% for B, and 44% for C. The actual weights for these positions at the end of day$_t$ were 29%, 34% and 38%, respectively. The actions computed, as the differences of the actual weights and the no-action weights on day$_t$, are an add of 4% for A, an add of 2% for B, and a trim of –6% for C. As this example demonstrates, computing actions is straightforward, and the results are both intuitive and analytically meaningful.

Table 5.1
Simple add and trim

Position	Day (t–1) Portfolio weight	Day (t) No-action weight	Portfolio weight	Action weight	Type
A	20%	25%	29%	4%	Add
B	30%	32%	34%	2%	Add
C	50%	44%	38%	–6%	Trim

The next example illustrates how a new buy and a sell or liquidation are computed.

This time the fund begins with four positions: A, B, C, and D as of the end of day$_{t-1}$, as depicted in table 5.2. During the next day position D is sold, resulting in it having a zero weight at the end of day$_t$. The proceeds from the sale of position D are reallocated as adds to positions A, B, and C plus funding the purchase of a new buy indicated as position E. Notice that the buy and sell actions are unique. The end-of-day weight of zero on day$_t$ indicates a sell or full liquidation, whereas going from a zero weight on day$_{t-1}$ to a non-zero weight on day$_t$ denotes a buy or the start of a new position.

Actual funds are more complicated, of course. They usually hold scores of positions—with even highly concentrated funds frequently holding twenty-five or more positions. Funds also hold some of their capital in cash, and many augment their stock holdings by investing in other security types, such as index-tracking mutual funds and electronically traded funds, sector specific ETFs, options, and short sell contracts. All of which means that the simple examples discussed here can quickly become computationally intense when applied to real-world funds.[2]

Additional Considerations

Not all actions are equal. For example, when considering a long-only fund, it is often preferred to limit the analysis of actions to only those positions with an active weight (i.e., portfolio weight greater than benchmark weight and/or nonbenchmark positions). This approach focuses the analysis on those positions reflecting active bets made by the manager. Sub-benchmark

Table 5.2
Basic buy and sell

Position	Day (t–1) Portfolio weight	Day (t) No action weight	Portfolio weight	Action weight	Type
A	20%	23%	25%	2%	Add
B	25%	20%	24%	4%	Add
C	30%	35%	36%	1%	Add
D	25%	22%	0%	−22%	Sell
E	0%	0%	15%	15%	Buy
	100%	100%	100%		

weight positions within a long-only fund are important, of course, as they help manage risk, initiate so-called starter positions, and limit tracking error. Yet by focusing exclusively on active weight positions, skill analyses rest squarely on the active decisions made by the manager—presumably, the choices that are intended to generate excess returns. Another useful refinement is the introduction of a materiality threshold. Tiny actions of a few basis points (+/−) rarely reflect the manager having rethought the alpha generating potential of an active position. Tiny actions can be the product of a number of portfolio management activities such as the short-term parking of cash (adds) disproportionally in a handful or so of the most liquid positions while waiting for the next buy opportunity, or the need to quickly raise funds from trims across highly liquid positions in order to satisfy a current modest capital requirement (i.e., strategic add). Setting a materiality threshold (i.e., minimum action size) enables the analysis to sidestep these nonstrategic actions, thus avoiding small weight changes that do not reflect efforts by the manager to meaningfully change the composition of the fund.

Action details for a single position are plotted in figure 5.1. The line graph indicates the position's return relative to its benchmark, using the y-axis on the left. The shaded background indicates the position's daily fund weight, using the y-axis on the right. The shaded dots denote each action. The initial buy and subsequent adds are indicated by the darker-shaded gray dots, while trims and the final sell are represented by the lighter-shaded gray dots.[3] The position shown was started in early 2018 with an initial weight of approximately 1%. The stock experienced a significant run-up in price (over 60%) shortly after purchase. The position then encountered a protracted (four-year) decline. During this time period, several adds and trims occurred, with one add pretty much at the bottom in 2022. The stock then rebounded with a few adds on the way up, with the stock ultimately pulling back to its initial purchase price by the end of the analysis.

From a decision perspective, this position could have been managed more effectively. Several adds were executed as the stock's price was falling. Other adds were made on the rebound, delivering some modest benefit to position results. There were two moments in history when this position could have been liquidated at a nice gain. Obviously, this did not happen. Instead, a growing amount of capital was tied up in this position for

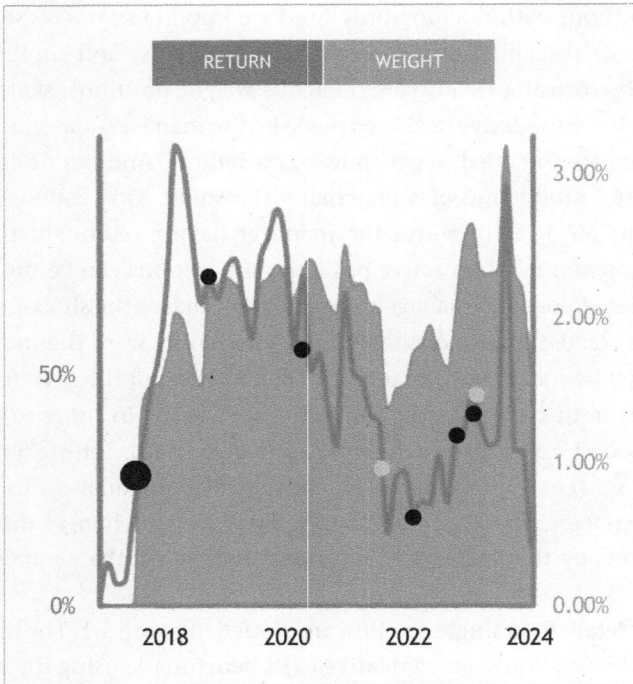

Figure 5.1
Visualizing actions.

approximately six years for a break-even relative return. The one add as the price bottomed out, however, was nicely executed.

The plotting of a single position is not sufficient information for drawing any conclusions about persistent strengths or shortcomings in decision-making. However, this limited information may spark a thought that, with further corroboration from other position visualizations and fund-level analyses, can lead to a stronger understanding of the skills associated with a current or new fund.

Takeaways. This analysis demonstrates how actions can be identified and plotted. Visualizing actions supports a deeper understanding of how skills relate to the management of individual positions. In doing so, these visualizations bridge the connection between rigorous analysis and anecdotal evidence. These plots also facilitate more effective discussions between capital allocators and the managers of the funds in which they invest.

Conclusion

Despite skill being the raison d'être for active equity management, it remains poorly understood. A great deal of the confusion regarding skill stems from the overreliance on conventional analytics, which use fund return series and holdings histories as their data inputs. The conventional metrics they generate provide weak proxies for skill. In contrast, analytics based on decisions provide more rigorous and useful indicators of skill. They do so by directly relating decisions to the results they help generate. Three prevalent methods for identifying decisions are trade data, position episodes, and actions. Each of these approaches is useful and provides more information about skills than is obtainable from conventional analytics.

Actions, which are used in the examples of newer analytics presented in subsequent chapters, are defined as the change in the weights of a fund's positions, from one day to the next, that cannot be explained by price movements alone. Therefore, actions represent decisions made intentionally by the manager to change the composition or bets within a fund. In addition to being used as a primary input into skill analyses, actions can be plotted to illustrate how individual positions are being managed. These visualizations provide a clear link between analytically generated skill results and how such skills affect day-to-day decision-making. The use of actions to generate counterfactual portfolios and then skills is discussed in the following two chapters.

6   The Value of Counterfactual Thinking

True intuitive expertise is learned from prolonged experience with good feedback on mistakes.
—Daniel Kahneman

Successful equity fund selection requires the kind of skill that can only be obtained from many years of experience in assessing funds and their managers. But not just any experience is sufficient. It requires experience that begins with rigorously developed insights into a fund's skills and investment processes. It then uses these same data and the fund's performance to calibrate how well today's allocation decisions play out over time. The importance of accurate skill information as inputs to developing the expert judgment necessary in making successful allocation decisions cannot be overstated. No amount of individual intelligence or diligence can overcome the deficiencies resulting from a poor understanding of a fund's true strengths and shortcomings.

Working with Counterfactuals

Counterfactuals, or more precisely counterfactual portfolio histories, facilitate the assessment of which of the fund's decisions add to fund results and which don't. They can be constructed to analyze relatively broad skills or decisions (e.g., buying) or narrowly defined skills (e.g., adds to winning positions with relatively high earnings growth). Counterfactual analyses calculate skills using scores, if not hundreds, of decisions (i.e., data points) regarding broad or narrow types of decisions. The results of counterfactual analyses, therefore, are robust and may be very specific.[1]

Conceptually, the way counterfactuals are constructed is to begin with a fund's actual history of daily holdings, and then apply an adjustment to the particular skill or decision being analyzed. Consider a fund that on occasion purchased stocks outside of its benchmark. To learn if these positions helped or hurt the actual fund's performance, a counterfactual would be constructed that eliminated all of the fund's buys of stocks outside of its benchmark. At each such buy, the counterfactual would essentially reverse the purchase (sell what had just been acquired), and then reallocate the sales proceeds on a pro rata basis to all of the other positions in the fund on that day. This two-step process eliminates the new (out of benchmark) buy and maintains the correct portfolio weights for the remaining positions. This same process is then applied to each such out-of-benchmark acquisition within the fund history being analyzed. The returns and relative returns for this counterfactual are then computed. If the actual fund outperforms the counterfactual, this indicates that owning the out-of-benchmark stocks helped fund returns. If the actual fund underperformed the counterfactual, this shows that owning the out-of-benchmark stocks hurt rather than helped fund results.

As is elaborated on below, computing the sizing skill is done by comparing the results of the actual fund to those of a counterfactual. The difference in results between two counterfactuals is used to compute the selling skill. The buying skill is computed directly from a single counterfactual. All three methods are used to quantify more granular skills (e.g., selling younger winners with relatively high earnings growth rates).

Focusing on Active Bets

Before proceeding, however, it is useful to first consider a refinement frequently involved in skill analysis. This involves adjusting only those fund positions with a positive active weight (i.e., fund weight greater than benchmark weight) when constructing counterfactuals. The rationale is that these active weight positions represent the bets made by the fund to generate excess returns. Generating excess returns is, of course, the purpose of active management and the ultimate skill being sought by capital allocators. Fund holdings outside the benchmark are active positions as well since, by definition, their total weight exceeds their benchmark weight. Below-benchmark weight positions are important as well since they help manage risk or represent potential alpha generators that have not yet received their full sizing. However, the purpose of below-benchmark weight positions is not explicitly to help generate excess returns. For this reason, the discussion below assumes using only active weight positions in computing skills.

Quantifying the Three Basic Skills

Measuring skill levels is a primary use of counterfactuals. This section describes, in conceptual terms, how the three basic manager skills are computed. Their order of presentation—first sizing, then buying, followed by selling—supports a highly intuitive progression of each counterfactual and the skill it quantifies.

Sizing Skill

The sizing skill is computed as the difference between the results of the actual fund and a counterfactual wherein the manager's actual buy and sell decisions are used but none of their sizing decisions. Sizing is instead accomplished using a passive rule. The preferred rule being to give each buy, at the time it goes active, the sum of its benchmark weight plus its equal share of the counterfactual portfolio's then total active weight (i.e., equal active weight), which together comprise the passive weight for a new buy.[2] The equal active weight for a single buy is computed as the fund's total active weight divided by the number of active positions held on the buy date, inclusive of the new buy being sized. For example, if the total active weight is 90% and the fund has forty-four active positions prior to the new buy, the equal active weight for a new buy would be 2% ($90\% \div 45 = 2\%$). The passive weight may be achieved over multiple days to reflect the fund's observed liquidity tolerance.[3]

Constructing the counterfactual to measure the sizing skill begins by copying the entire fund history. Then, starting with the first buy (i.e., the date that the first position achieves an active weight), a series of adjustments are made. First, from the date of the position's buy to the day it is sold, the position's entire weight history is deleted. In place of its actual daily weights the position receives on the date of the initial buy its passive weight (benchmark plus equal active weight). From then on, its daily active weight will be driven by the return of the position relative to the total return of the counterfactual portfolio. Should the position outperform the counterfactual, its active weight will increase. Likewise, should the position underperform the counter factual, its weight will decrease. The result is a single counterfactual position whose active buy and sell dates mirror those in the actual fund, but whose initial active weight is established using a passive sizing rule and whose weight thereafter is influenced by the position's performance relative to the counterfactual. The same adjustments are then made to all other active positions in the fund being analyzed.

For each buy thus adjusted, its passive weight can be greater than, less than, or equal to its weight in the actual fund (i.e., its fund weight). When the passive weight for a position is greater than its fund weight, the additional capital for the buy is obtained by a pro rata trim of all other positions in the fund on the buy date.[4] When the passive weight is less than the fund weight, the surplus capital is redeployed by adding the difference pro rata across all the other positions in the fund. Naturally, no adjustments are necessary if the passive weight equals the fund weight.

It's also possible for positions to experience reverse or offsetting adjustments essentially on top of each other. For example, consider position XYZ, which may one day be trimmed along with other fund positions in order to accommodate the purchase of buy ABC, whose passive weight is larger than its fund weight. Subsequently, on the same day position XYZ, along with all other fund positions, might receive an add when position ABC is purchased and its passive weight is less than its fund weight. This truing up after each buy is passively sized allows the counterfactual to mirror the overall total active weight and construction parameters of the actual fund. When completed, this counterfactual will contain all of the manager's active buy and sell decisions but none of the manager's active sizing decisions. This particular form of counterfactual is termed the "name portfolio" because on every single day it contains every stock (name) held in the actual fund, although sized passively.

The daily returns and annualized relative returns are then computed for the name portfolio. The manager's overall skill in position sizing is computed as the difference between the relative return of the actual fund and the name portfolio. A positive difference indicates the manager is, in aggregate, skilled at sizing, meaning that the net effect of their active sizing decisions outperformed a passive approach. A negative difference indicates the manager is not particularly skilled at sizing—their active sizing decisions in aggregate underperforming a passive rule. This comparison of the fund's results to those of a uniquely developed counterfactual provides clear insight into the manager's overall sizing skill. The sizing skill can then be investigated more granularly, as discussed later on in this chapter.

Takeaways. A positive sizing skill indicates that the fund is capturing a significant amount, if not all, of the alpha available from its buys, subject to its own construction and risk rules. The more positive the fund's sizing skill, the better its chances at generating consistent results, all things being equal. A negative sizing skill may alert the capital allocator that additional investigation into sizing is warranted. Some of the questions that might then be addressed include: Are a few really bad years responsible for the negative results, or is sizing consistently challenged? Are the negative results a more recent phenomenon or more historic? Are winning positions being built up effectively, or is alpha being lost due to anemic sizing? Do adds and trims help generate excess returns, or do they destroy it? Answers to questions like these enable the capital allocator to discern whether the sizing skill is consistently strong, persistently challenged, or volatile.

Buy Skill

The buy skill is computed using a single counterfactual. This one is based on the name portfolio developed above. Starting with a copy of the name portfolio, all of the actual sell decisions are then replaced with passive selling. The result is a counterfactual that reflects the buy decisions of the actual fund with passive sizing and passive selling. Because only the fund's active buy decisions are being analyzed, this counterfactual is referred to as the "buy portfolio." This counterfactual enables the analysis to focus exclusively on the alpha generating ability of the manager's stock picking. There are several methods for effecting passive selling.[5] The approach discussed here involves selling positions based on a method referred to as first in, first out (FIFO). This passive sell approach results in a buy portfolio that is highly respectful of (or mirrors) the manager's actual fund construction and governance. Meaning that on each day the counterfactual reflects the same number of positions held, turnover rate, and total active share as the actual fund.

Here is how FIFO selling is implemented: On each day when a position is sold in the actual fund, the counterfactual portfolio sells its then oldest position. Therefore, the buy portfolio is selling a different position than was sold from the actual fund pretty much every time. Consequently, some positions are sold from the buy portfolio sooner than they were sold from the actual fund (i.e., their sell is advanced), while others are sold from the buy portfolio after they were sold from the actual fund (i.e., their sell is delayed). Selling based on the FIFO approach does necessitate tracking the daily age of all active positions in the buy portfolio. Each liquidation commences on its sell date and is completed over as many days as required to match the fund's liquidity tolerance.

The result is a counterfactual portfolio that buys exactly what the actual fund buys commencing on the same day (uses the manager's active buy decision); sizes passively (based on an equal active weight rule); and sells passively (using a FIFO approach). This counterfactual isolates the manager's active buy decisions from their other active management decisions. It provides a clear measure of the fund's ability to identify alpha generating stocks. Once constructed, the daily returns for the buy portfolio can be computed. The annualized relative return of this buy portfolio quantifies the magnitude of the buy skill.

Takeaways. Generating excess returns consistently is difficult. It is made all the more so absent a strong buy skill. It's possible to deliver benchmark-beating results with a modest or weak buy skill. But doing so requires impeccable skill in both selling and sizing to make up for lackluster buying. Funds with strong buy skills enjoy more latitude in making some mistakes or facing challenging market conditions and still exceeding or coming close to the returns of their benchmarks. A consistent information advantage together with a meaningfully positive buy skill are metrics that help capital allocators who are looking for repeatable success. Questions that commonly arise from examining the overall buy skill include: Is the buy skill consistent over time or highly volatile? Is the fund able to make strong buys across all sectors and/or global regions? Is the nature of the buys (i.e., factor signature) reflective of the fund's stated strategy and style? Analytics that answer these questions are described in future chapters.

Sell Skill

The sell skill is computed as the difference between the name portfolio and the buy portfolio. This identity reflects the following algebraic resolution:

1. The name portfolio contains both active buying and active selling, with sizing accomplished passively; and
2. The buy portfolio contains only active buying, with both sizing and selling implemented passively; therefore

3. The difference between these two counterfactuals equals the impact of the fund's active sell decisions or sell skill.

Elaborating on the above, the name portfolio and the buy portfolio each contain the fund's active buy skill; therefore, computing the difference between these two values cancels this term. Similarly, the name portfolio and the buy portfolio each contain passive sizing; therefore, computing the difference between the two values cancels this term as well. The sole component on which the two portfolios contain different values is selling. The name portfolio contains the fund's active sell decisions while the buy portfolio contains passive selling. Consequently, the difference between these two portfolios is the impact of active selling versus passive selling—the sell skill.

Takeaway. Selling tends to be the least developed skill among active equity managers. While a positive skill is desired, many managers are able to generate consistently strong excess returns so long as the drag or negative impact from the sell skill is smaller than the positive impacts of the combined buy and sizing skills. When the sell skill is negative, capital allocators then want to understand if selling been a consistent drag on the fund or if something has changed recently. Might there be reason to suspect that selling is becoming even less effective and is likely to do more harm to fund results going forward?

Taking a Granular Look

A closer look at each skill is available through more granular investigations. Such investigations may consider looking at a skill across smaller and perhaps consecutive time periods (e.g., year-by-year), narrowly defined skills (e.g., the selling of older positions), isolating decisions by stock attribute or factor (e.g., buys of stocks with relatively high return on investment), or the cross-section of these qualities (e.g., adds to older positions that are winners, exhibiting above median cash flow on invested capital, for the most recent three years and the three-year period immediately preceding). Reviewing skills over a range of time periods informs just how consistently a skill adds to or detracts from fund results. The analysis of narrowly defined skills may point to a relatively small number of choices that are having an outsized impact on results. Investigations by sector or global region can point to staff/process weaknesses that can be discussed with the manager and fund team. Skill results computed by factor can help confirm that the fund is being managed in accordance to its stated strategy and style.

Additional Counterfactuals

The counterfactuals described thus far are constructed to assess overall skills with varying levels of granularity. The additional analyses below address questions that are regularly posed during fund due diligence and/or manager interviews.

Sell timing.   Selling is not one skill but a host of specific skills. A sell can be too early or too late. And the sell timing may be more effective for positions with unrealized gains ("winners") or unrealized losses ("losers"). Examining sell timing, therefore, involves constructing four distinct counterfactuals, one each to assess skill in selling: younger winners, younger losers, older winners, and older losers. A fund may have a positive overall sell skill yet give away significant alpha by not selling older winners in a timely manner. Similarly, a fund may exhibit an overall negative sell skill while the sell timing analysis indicates that the problem lies predominantly in selling young winners too quickly (i.e., not capturing their full alpha). The results of sell timing, together with other sell-related analytics, provide deep insight into the strengths and shortcomings of a fund's harvesting of positions. More about sell timing is presented in chapter 9.

Stop loss.   A stop-loss analysis investigates how effectively substantial losers are being managed. This analysis involves constructing multiple counterfactuals that sell off positions as they meet or exceed distinct loss thresholds, such as down 20%, down 30%, and down 40%. The results indicate the impact on the fund's relative return had the affected positions been sold as they hit each of the loss thresholds. This analysis describes how effectively the fund is managing its substantial losers and quantifies how much alpha, if any, is being lost to a likely process flaw. Stop-loss analysis is explored in chapter 11.

Initial sizing.   Great buys can give their full alpha to the fund only when they are effectively sized before taking off. Assessing how well the fund's stronger buys are being sized involves constructing multiple counterfactuals that bring undersized winners up to full position weight sooner than occurred in the actual fund. Slow buildup may reflect a process flaw or uncertain conviction. The analysis of ramping up new buys is discussed in chapter 12.

Takeaways. Additional counterfactuals can provide important insights that relate directly to fund assessment. Results from these additional counterfactuals corroborate insights from other counterfactual investigations. They also provide orthogonal assessments of risk (e.g., stop loss) that are strongly additive to conventional analytics.

Conclusion

Fund selection is a highly skilled profession. Developing the requisite skills requires not just experience but the right kind of experience—where expert judgment and decision processes are honed with the aid of accurate information. Counterfactuals are one of a set of newer analytics that provide direct quantification of the skills driving a fund's results. Conceptually straightforward, the counterfactual isolates a series of similar decisions made, and then adjusts or modulates those decisions to determine their impact on fund outcomes. Counterfactuals are then used to compute specific skills. Positive skill values indicate that, on average, the manager's decisions are adding value. Negative skill values reflect that, in general, the manager's decisions are hurting rather than helping fund returns.

Counterfactuals are used in measuring skills in aggregate (i.e., buying, selling, and sizing) as well as investigating skills more granularly (e.g., across time periods, by sector, or by factor). Specific counterfactuals directly support fund due diligence by assessing the management of substantial losers, the timeliness of building winners to full size, and the timing of selling winners and losers.

Counterfactual results are highly complementary with those provided by conventional analytics. Together, the results of these newer analytics and those of conventional analytics provide capital allocators with a clearer understanding of manager skill and a stronger assessment of the fund's likelihood of delivering benchmark-beating results going forward.

A good decision is based on knowledge and not on numbers.
—Plato

The presence and magnitude of skill cannot be distilled down to a single number or even a handful of them. Instead, skill assessment requires judgment. Specifically, it involves expert judgment applied to synthesizing and evaluating a variety of rigorously developed skill metrics. This includes metrics that measure the alpha contribution of a skill, its persistence, its prevalence across sectors and financial factors, and its durability over time and market cycles. Exercising judgments based on measures like these can help identify which active equity funds are more likely to deliver excess returns going forward.

Starting with the Basics

Consider an actual fund that generated a relative return of 8.36% over a nine-year period. Such a fund seems worth further investigation. Using conventional analytics, it's possible to learn more about the fund's results, such as annual return volatility, fund composition, upside/downside capture, and a variety of risk metrics. These are highly informative pieces of information but do not help assess how likely this fund is to continue outperforming, as discussed in chapter 3. In order to really understand the future potential of this fund, it is helpful to examine the skills and investment processes that are driving its results.

An initial skill investigation might begin with a look at the three basic skills of buying, selling, and sizing. Results for these three basic skills are

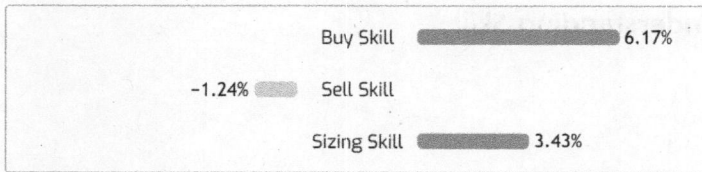

Figure 7.1
Three basic skills.

presented in figure 7.1. Both the buy skill and sizing skills are positive at 6.17% and 3.43%, respectively. The selling skill is a headwind for the fund's returns at −1.24%.[1] It is not uncommon for an outperforming fund to exhibit at least one negative skill. What's important for handicapping future success is that the positive skills are sufficiently large so as to more than offset the negative skill, that there is little reason to believe that the positive skills are likely to decline significantly, and that there is no expectation that the negative skill will substantially worsen. A granular investigation to suss out these insights can start with any of the basic skills. To illustrate how granular investigations are used to provide deeper insight into skills, the following discussion provides a closer look at this fund's buy skill.

Investigating the Buy Skill

The buy skill quantifies the alpha generating capacity of the fund's typical active position, or what can be thought of as the manager's stock-picking ability. It reflects the judgment and investment processes contained in the new active buys initiated over a specific time period, when such buys are passively sized and passively sold (see chapter 6). A positive buy skill indicates that, on average, the purchases initiated over the analysis outperformed their benchmark and vice versa.

The 6.17% buy skill is clearly driving the fund's success. Given its importance, it would be valuable to know the consistency of this skill. There are many paths for investigating consistency. Looking at results year by year, by sector, and relative to financial attributes represent reasonable next steps.

Takeaways. The fund's excellent relative return is being driven by an impressive buy skill. Given the importance of the buy skill to fund success, it makes sense to next explore the consistency of this skill.

Annual Buy Skill

Year-by-year values of the fund's buy skill are presented in figure 7.2. The annual results indicate that the manager's buy skill varies considerably. The positive values range from 0.48% (2014) to 21.48% (2015). The single negative value is substantial at −7.25% in 2019. These results are less favorable than if the annual skill returns were more evenly distributed (i.e., smaller standard deviation), even if one or two more years were negative or close to zero. The volatility in annual buy skill results gives pause to assuming that buying prowess will continue to drive fund results.

Takeaways. Although the fund's average buy skill is strong, the year-by-year results expose a significant level of annual volatility. Further investigations are required in order to more fully understand the repeatability of the fund's buying skill going forward. Examining the fund's buy skill across sectors is considered next.

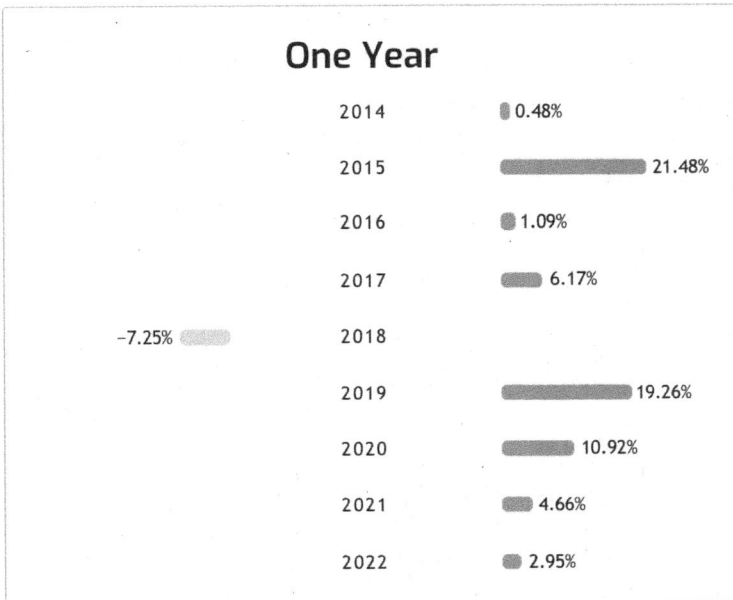

Figure 7.2
Annual buy skills.

Buy Skill by Sector

The fund's buy skill is positive in seven of eleven sectors, as shown in figure
7.3. Consumer staples have the strongest buy skill at 1.91% while consumer
discretionary exhibits the lowest buy skill at −1.68%.[2] Divergent skills across
sectors sometimes are structural in that they reflect varying analyst abilities
or differences in the research process from one sector to another. If this were
the case, then it is possible that the five sectors with negative buy skills
may be important contributors to the volatility observed within the annual
buy skills. A look at which sectors were heavily represented in the stock
purchases within years of strong buy skill versus weak buy skill could help
determine if this hypothesis is correct.

Takeaways. The fund is challenged in its buying across five sectors. It's
unclear whether this is due to the judgments of the research analyst or
shortcomings in the research processes. It's also possible that the manager

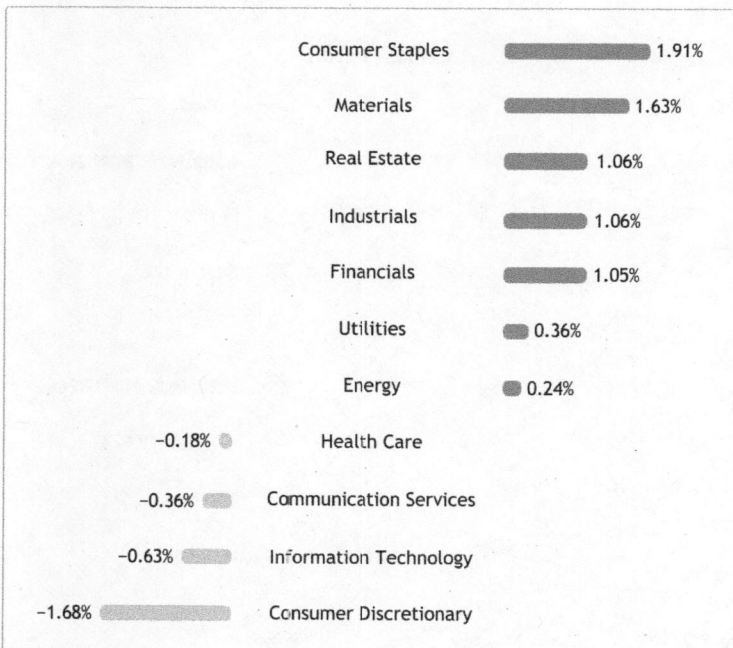

Consumer Staples 1.91%
Materials 1.63%
Real Estate 1.06%
Industrials 1.06%
Financials 1.05%
Utilities 0.36%
Energy 0.24%
−0.18% Health Care
−0.36% Communication Services
−0.63% Information Technology
−1.68% Consumer Discretionary

Figure 7.3
Buy skill by sector.

or investment committee may be engaging in adverse selection with regard to these sectors (i.e., selecting the weakest recommendations from the sector analysts). This latter question can sometimes be addressed by comparing the results of the "analyst paper portfolios" (constructed from each analysts' recommendations) to the fund's actual returns by sector.

What is now known is that the fund's buy skill is volatile and this skill is weak across five sectors. A look at buying based on the relative levels of financial attributes at the time of initial purchase is considered next.

Buy Skill by Financial Attribute

Funds frequently seek out stocks with distinct financial characteristics or attribute signatures. Among fundamental managers, such characteristics often involve traditional factors and analysts stock ranks.[3] When quantitative screening is used, the attributes can include multifactor regression results (so-called alpha scores) along with traditional factors. Attribute analyses offer insight into which financial characteristics or recommendations (and their levels) are most associated with a fund's successful and unsuccessful new buys.

The efficacy or alpha generation of the fund's buys, which at the time of the initial acquisition reflected relatively weak or strong balance sheet quality (i.e., relatively high or low debt-to-asset ratios), is presented in figure 7.4. New buys with weaker balance sheet quality at time of initial purchase fared better for this fund. These buys generated 8.01% relative return annually. In contrast, the buys with higher balance sheet quality generated a −1.67% relative return over the same period. The divergence in outcome based on relative balance sheet quality may speak to the fund having a value tilt regarding its style and the types of stocks pursued and/or most effectively researched. This observation might support the notion that the fund

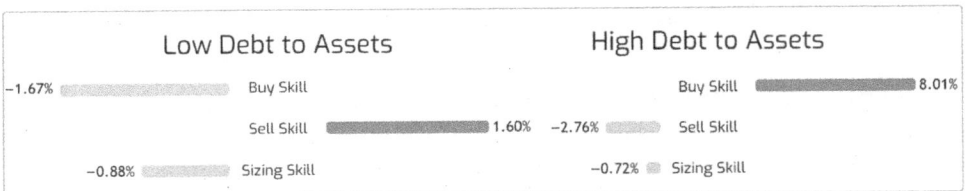

	Low Debt to Assets		High Debt to Assets	
Buy Skill	−1.67%			8.01%
Sell Skill		1.60%	−2.76%	
Sizing Skill	−0.88%		−0.72%	

Figure 7.4
Buy skills by financial attribute.

makes its strongest purchases with companies that are relatively highly leveraged. As it is often expressed by fund managers: "The fund does well when buying companies with a little hair on the balance sheet."

Takeaways. The fund's buys with relatively lower balance sheet quality outperform buys with relatively higher balance sheet quality. This same type of analysis can be repeated for other financial attributes (i.e., earnings, valuation, momentum). These results help assess which attributes are associated with the fund's strongest and weakest buys. They also help confirm if the fund's description of what's driving results is actually represented in the stocks being purchased.

What's Been Learned

Past performance is widely used as a critical threshold for identifying which funds are advanced to receive further analysis. In the example above, the fund's relative return is impressive at 8.36%. And this measure seemed even more impressive in that it represented the average over a nine-year history. A look at the fund's three basic skills indicates that the results are being driven primarily by strong buying, helped some by sizing, and clearly dampened by negative selling. Initial granular investigations into the buy skill showed that it is highly volatile from year to year, ineffective in five of eleven sectors, and works best when focused on stocks with relatively weak balance sheets. While definitely informative and offering reasons for caution concerning the likely persistence of the fund's outperformance, the results so far are not yet conclusive. Further granular skill investigations are needed before a definitive judgment about this fund's desirability can be formulated. Yet even this partial dive into the fund's skills clearly demonstrates the vast improvement in understanding that is attainable using the newer analytics. They provide tremendous insight into which decisions are helping to lift fund results (or not) and their consistency.

A Brief Look at Selling and Sizing Skills

Each of the analyses reviewed thus far can be performed for selling and sizing as well. Figure 7.4 includes the results of relatively high and low balance sheet quality for all three basic skills. Much like the buy skill, the results for the fund indicate that the sizing of positions with relatively low balance sheet quality outperforms the sizing of positions with relatively higher balance sheet quality. This finding might be construed as consistent with the buy results in that both the purchase of and allocation of additional capital to relatively high leveraged companies seems to work well for this fund. The signs reverse when this attribute is used to assess selling skill. Here the selling of higher balance sheet quality positions outperforms the selling of lower balance sheet quality positions. This could be interpreted as suggesting the higher balance sheet quality positions are being sold once they have realized their thesis and are no longer value stocks. Whereas the lower quality balance sheet positions are sold perhaps because they were simply poor buys or never realized their thesis. It's plainly observable that lining up financial attributes with decisions (i.e., buying, selling, and sizing) can substantially enrich the assessment of how a fund's excess returns are being generated.

Takeaways. The fund's sizing skill diverges based on relative debt-to-asset ratios. Buying and sizing proved strongest for lower quality balance sheets stocks, whereas selling was most effective with positions reflecting higher balance sheet quality. It may be informative to investigate if this financial attribute is an explicit element of the fund's investment processes as well as considering additional financial attributes.

Multiple Time Periods

Thus far skills have been examined over long time periods and year by year. The former is valuable, of course, but may conceal undesirable trends or erratic interim results, as was identified above. The latter provides useful granularity yet may be difficult to internalize as to whether the results are generally good or not. This is where multiyear results can help. They deliver more granularity than a single value for the entire history being analyzed while smoothing out some of the noisiness that can accompany measures that are year-by-year. The following presents multiyear results for a different fund. This one reflects an unfavorable sizing skill.

Figure 7.5 shows the fund's sizing skill measured in three consecutive three-year periods. The sizing skill values are -3.54%, 2.76%, and -3.60%, for the three time periods. These results reflect a net negative sizing skill and a good bit of volatility as well. Further disheartening is that the result for the most recent three-year period is negative. These results offer little reason to suspect that the fund can depend upon sizing to bolster returns going

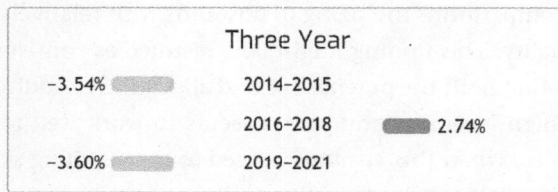

Three Year		
-3.54%	2014–2015	
	2016–2018	2.74%
-3.60%	2019–2021	

Figure 7.5
Rolling sizing skills.

forward. If anything, the inconsistent results and recent spate of negative sizing impacts render this skill more a source of risk than excess returns.

Takeaways. Consecutive multiyear analyses provide a helpful complement to the historical average and year-by-year results in any skill investigation. These consecutive multiyear results highlight the presence or absence of skill consistencies.

Conclusion

Identifying equity management skill is a difficult task. Ultimately it relies upon human judgment. This judgment is both refined and utilized best with the support of robust skill metrics.

The analyses presented explore various dimensions of skill with the use of actions and counterfactual portfolios (described in the two previous chapters). The analytics introduced include measuring the three basic skills, quantifying skills over varying time periods, evaluating skills across sectors, and assessing skill strength with regard to relatively high and low levels of financial attributes.

Results across the various investigations provide a highly valuable interim assessment of the fund's buy skill. Specifically, the investigations highlight the historic strength of the buy skill while calling into question its ability to drive fund results going forward. The analysis highlights how the newer analytics deliver skill insights that are not available from conventional analytics.

Skill analytics have improved over the past decade or so, as demonstrated herein. The use of the newer analytics, however, is not yet widespread. Greater adoption of these newer analytics represents a clear path for enhancing skill assessment and ultimately making more effective equity investments by all manner of capital allocator.

8 The Buy Process

The process is the foundation of success. Trust it, embrace it, and let it guide you towards greatness.

—John Addison

Identifying repeatability is a central goal in fund searches. Particularly when it involves repeatability of decisions that generate strong results. A robust process for selecting stocks to purchase can help provide the type of repeatability desired. Such a buy process would guide the manager toward potential new stocks for the fund that are likely alpha generators and that are aligned with the fund's proven judgment and research efforts. The buy process would also ensure that potential new buys are well matched to the fund's strategy and style. No doubt most managers believe they have and use such a process. And some actually do. Discerning if a particular fund does have a clear buy process, and if it is helpful and used regularly, is not easily done. Today, the active equities industry operates mostly devoid of such basic information. Overcoming this deficit can add meaningfully to the fund assessment process and help improve allocation decisions.

Putting Buys Into Context

A fund's ability to deliver benchmark-beating results is severely limited absent great buys. Regularly making successful buys, however, is extremely difficult. Accurately explaining how it is being done is even harder, if not impossible, using conventional approaches. The prevailing means of describing a buy process involves a few bullet points on a slide. This is usually accompanied by several anecdotes and a statement of guiding principles. This information may or may not reflect what actually happens when new stocks are purchased. Even if it is fairly accurate, which is more unlikely than not, there is no analytic verification to support what is being presented. Fortunately, there are newer methods for computing what types of stocks a fund is actually purchasing. The results of the newer analytics are data-driven and do not rely upon promotional materials, the manager's recollections, or research analyst notes. The newer buy process descriptors are completely data-driven. They explain what kind of stocks are actually being purchased. Not surprisingly, what's being purchased is often very different from what is intended or what the manager may believe.

One such method for assessing a fund's buys is termed "context analysis." It facilitates the analytic expression of a fund's buy process based on the financial characteristics of the stocks being purchased, as of the day of initial buy. Context analysis answers the question: Exactly what kind of stocks is the fund purchasing on average? The answer consists of the most descriptive financial characteristics or attributes and their relative levels.[1] For example, a fund may tend to buy stocks with well-above-average margin growth, below-average leverage, and above-average price momentum. In other words, these attributes and their relative amounts describe the fund's typical new buy (also referred to as the "attribute signature" of the typical new buy). This description portrays the endpoint of the buy process. Just how such a characterization of a buy process is constructed is described next.

Anatomy of a Buy

Context analysis begins with constructing a normalized, sector-relative daily history of attribute values for all stocks in the fund's investable universe.[2] The first part of constructing this history is to compute the daily sector-relative attribute values for all stocks. This involves, on each day, dividing the actual value of every stock attribute by its corresponding sector median value.

Consider this example. Company XYZ is in the financial sector. On day one of the period being analyzed, the return on invested capital (ROIC) of company XYZ is divided by the median value of ROIC for the financial sector on that same day. When a stock's attribute value is larger than its sector median, the resulting value is greater than 1.0. Conversely, when a stock's attribute value is smaller than its sector median, the resulting value is less than 1.0. Negative sector-relative results are possible since stock attributes such as price momentum and earnings growth can have negative values. The same division described is then performed for company XYZ across all other attributes being considered. Then this same process is applied to all stocks in the investable universe. Finally, all of the calculations just described for day one are then repeated for the remaining days in the history being analyzed (i.e., day_2 to day_n). The end results are sector-relative values for all attributes, covering all stocks, across each day.

The next step involves normalizing the sector-relative values into percentiles. When completed, the sector medians are represented as the fiftieth percentile (or midpoint) with the lowest value representing the first percentile and the highest value representing the one-hundredth percentile. This normalized, sector-relative daily history of attribute values ("adjusted attribute history") facilitates meaningful comparisons of attribute values across sectors. For example, the level of debt for the typical financial sector company tends to be much greater than that for the typical information technology sector company. Yet it is helpful to understand if, in purchasing companies in either sector, the fund is buying those with high or low levels of debt relative to their sector peers (i.e., the attribute data is sector-neutralized). This adjusted attribute history data is then used to assess the financial characteristics of the fund's buys over time.

Next, the adjusted attribute history values are identified for each buy. For example, if the fund purchased stock XYZ on January 30, 2025, and this stock is within the retail durables sector, then its attribute values (for as many attributes being considered) would be chosen from the adjusted attribute history for that sector and day.[3] This same process is repeated for all buys present in the fund history. The results are adjusted attribute historical values for all buys being analyzed.

The final step involves determining which group of attributes most accurately describes the fund's average new stock purchase. Typical buy process descriptors contain between three and five attributes. In determining the most descriptive group, it is common to consider many potential attributes (generally between eight and fifteen). Each combination considered contains distinct sets of attributes and their levels. For example, a combination might be comprised of below-median leverage (debt-to-enterprise value), median price momentum (two-year average), and above-median financial performance (earnings growth). Each combination is evaluated to determine its correlation with all of the fund's buys using the least square statistical procedure. This analysis requires an enormous amount of computational power. The search can be streamlined, however, with the use of a machine learning algorithm known as hill climbing.[4] Each result is then ranked based on its level of correlation.

Upon completion the analysis identifies the set of attributes and their relative levels that best describe the types of stocks being purchased by the fund. This result is, in all respects, an analytic representation of the fund's buy process. The results can be plotted to provide a highly intuitive visualization of a fund's buy process. The insights available from using context analysis are discussed next.

Interpreting the Buy Context Plot

This section provides several examples of how context analysis is used to better understand what is being purchased by a fund and which types of buys are generating the strongest results.

The buy context for a global growth fund is presented in figure 8.1. The solid gray lines are the axes for the four attributes in this example. Where they meet in the middle is the lowest attribute value (first percentile). The outermost edge of each axis is the highest attribute value (hundredth percentile). The attributes in this buy context are sales growth, five-year earnings per share (EPS) growth, one-year price volatility, and three-year return. A thin gray line connects each axis at its midpoint, denoting the median values. The lightly shaded area (gray) in the background denotes the range (lowest to highest) of each attribute observed across the fund's entire set of buys over the history being analyzed. In this example the lower end of the range is fairly close to the first percentile for all attributes except for three-year returns, which is closer to the fifteenth percentile. Whereas the higher end of the range is roughly the eightieth percentile for all attributes. This rather broad range across attributes indicates that, while the fund may be targeting stocks of a specific character, it nevertheless is at least occasionally purchasing stocks whose attribute values are at both extremes.

The attribute signatures for the fund's winning and losing buys are indicated by the thick bold black line and the thick bold black dotted line, respectively. As used here, the term *winner* refers to a position that since

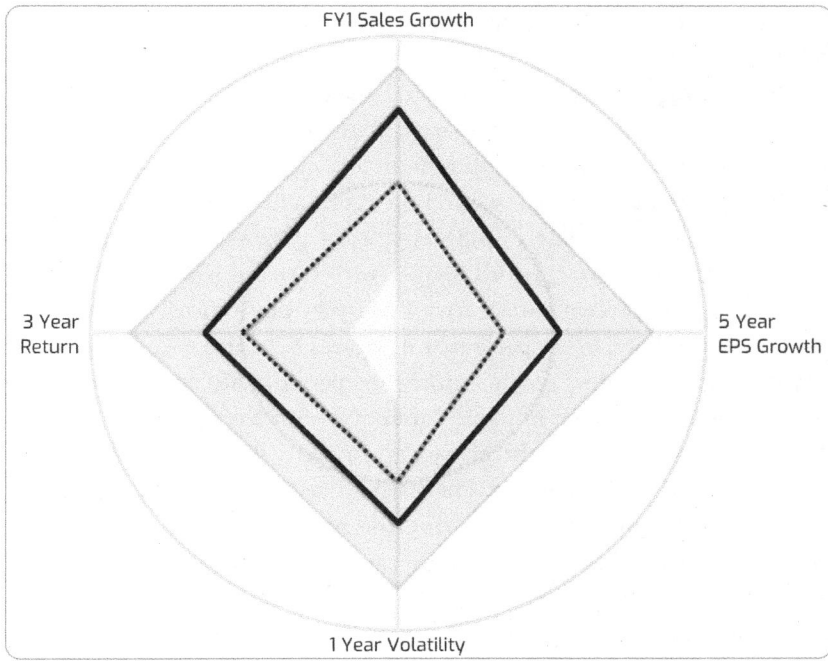

Figure 8.1
When more is better.

its initial purchase has gone on to outperform its sector average. Likewise, the term *loser* refers to a position that since its initial purchase has gone on to underperform its sector average. Figure 8.1 shows that the fund's winning buys tend to have relatively high levels of all attributes at time of initial purchase. The funds' losing buys, in contrast, tend to reflect attribute values much closer to their sector medians. Sizable differences like these indicate that both the levels and the attributes themselves are important to identifying strong stocks for this fund. Had the manager been aware of these results, it may have led the fund to focus its stock selection even more toward higher attribute value names.

Takeaways. The first observation is that the fund's buy context reflects a growth tilt based on the attribute types selected. This confirms that the fund is seeking new buys that fit its style and strategy. On average new buys tend to have attribute values at or above sector median. The average values for both winners and losers being above the median informs this inference.

Nevertheless, the fund does buy some stocks with attribute values below and well below the median (indicated by the range). These low-attribute-level buys, it might be surmised, may not be helping overall fund returns, given that its winners reflect higher attribute levels. Knowing what types of stocks a fund is actually buying provides highly valuable information concerning investment processes and the repeatability of results.

It is often useful to view a fund's buy process across multiple time periods. Consistency of process or changes within it are readily identifiable with this approach. Two consecutive three-year buy process diagrams for the growth fund above are presented in figures 8.2a and 8.2b. Figure 8.2a provides the buy context for the initial time period. The context analysis is fairly consistent with that in figure 8.1 above, with a couple of exceptions. The lowest range level for three-year return shifts from the fifteenth percentile to the fiftieth percentile. The attribute levels for winners and losers appear closer together as well. During the more recent three-year period presented in figure 8.2b, the minimum range value for three-year return is back to the fifteenth percentile, while the minimum range value for three-year EPS has shifted up to the fiftieth percentile. The average attribute values for winners and losers are essentially overlapping for one-year volatility, and the differences in the averages are a bit smaller for five-year EPS growth.

Takeaways. The buy contexts for the two time periods are generally consistent. This bodes well for the repeatability of stock selection going forward. One observation is that the average attribute values for winners and losers seem closer together in the initial three-year period relative to the more recent three-year period. This may be the result of market shifts over the two time periods (i.e., dispersion of attribute values) or a subtle shift in the types of stocks being targeted by the fund. This difference might be a discussion topic when meeting with the manager.

The results presented in figures 8.3a and 8.3b offer a very different story. It's obvious that this is a different fund, with a different set of buy attributes. It's also apparent that this fund is now targeting different types of stocks than it had earlier. The range of attribute values in figure 8.3a all begin at or are close to the first percentile and extend mostly up to the fiftieth percentile—the one exception being three-year sales growth reaching the eightieth percentile. The average attribute levels are fairly close together for winners and losers, with the exception of one-year returns. The winner and loser attribute levels for cash-flow yield, one-year volatility, and one-year return are at or

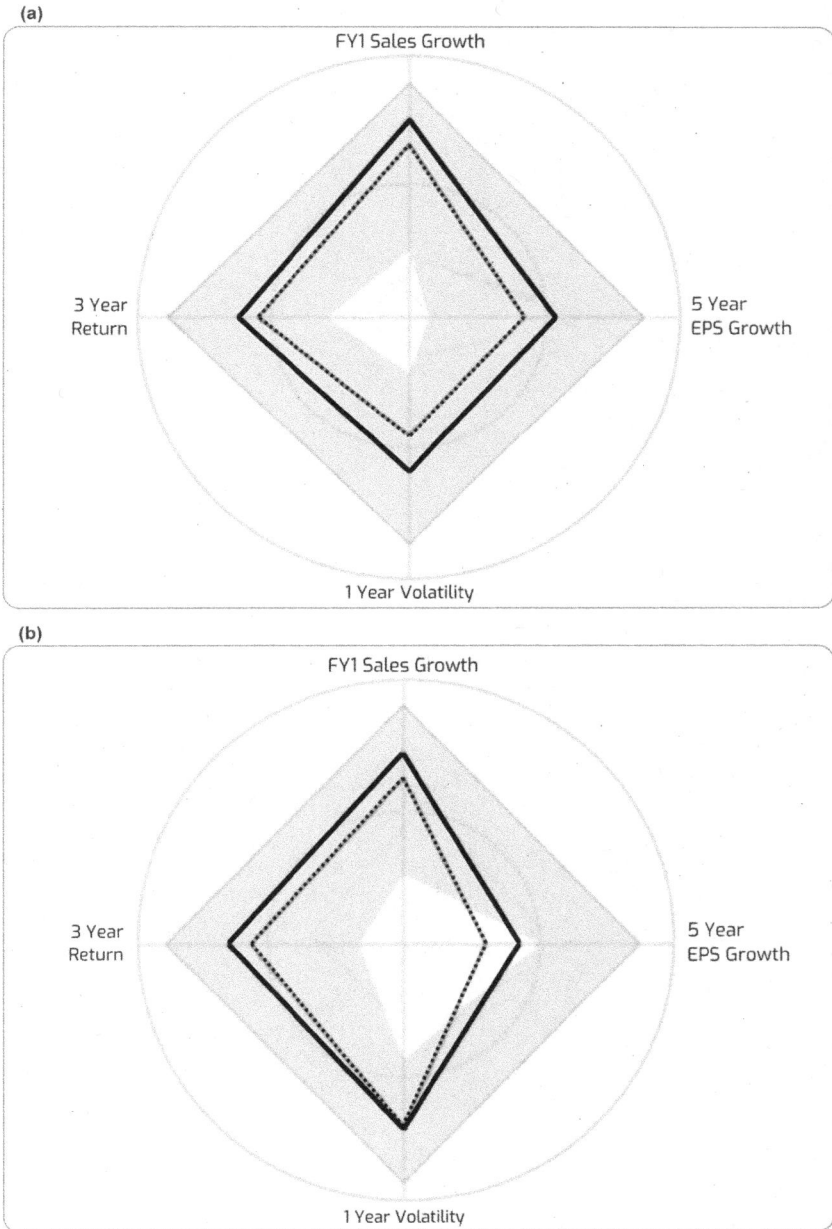

Figure 8.2
Looking for consistency.

(a)

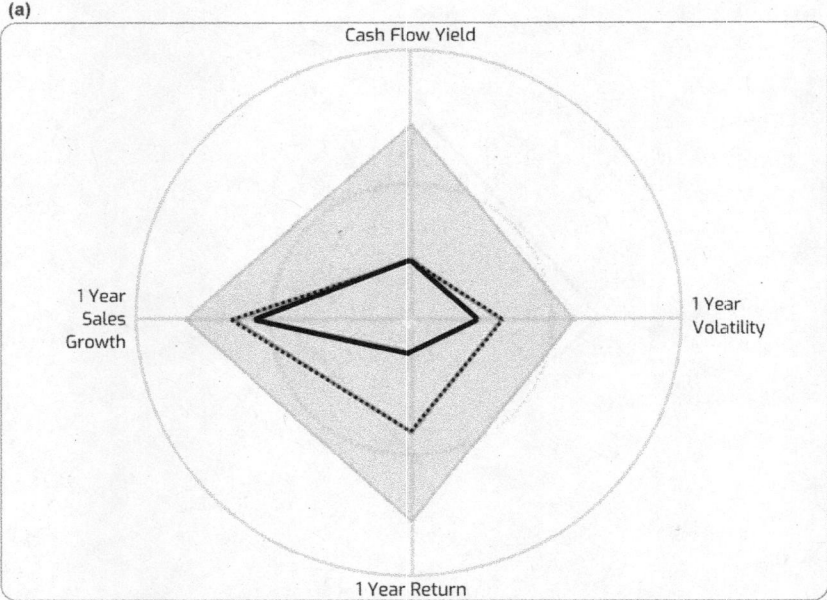

(b)

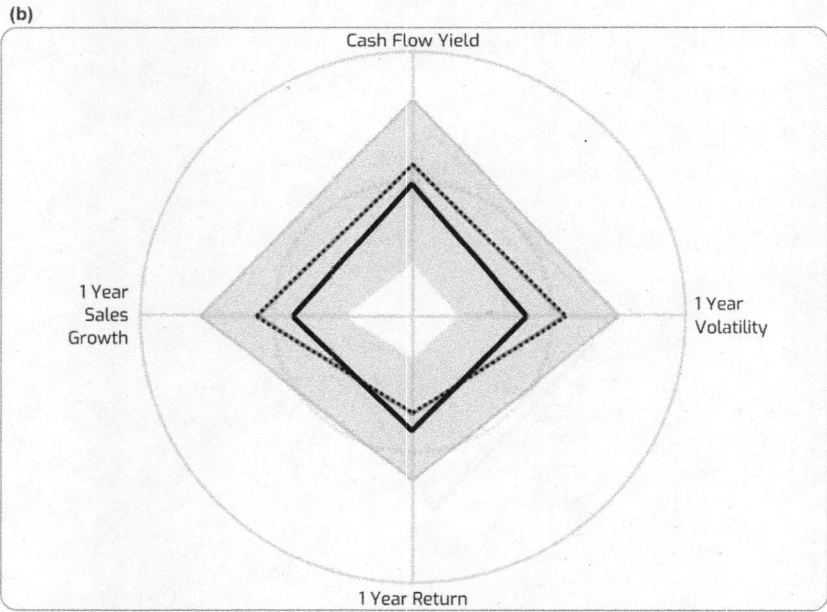

Figures 8.3
Changing process.

significantly below median, while both the winner and loser attribute levels for one-year sales growth are among the highest percentiles. The range in figure 8.3b has shifted slightly higher with minimum levels as high as the twentieth percentile, extending up to the seventieth and eightieth percentiles more recently. The average attribute levels for cash-flow yield and one-year volatility shifted higher (closer to median) for both winners and losers. The average winner level for one-year return shifted up from roughly the tenth percentile to the fiftieth percentile. The levels of one-year sales growth declined from the seventieth and eightieth quintiles to the fortieth and fiftieth quintiles for winners and losers, respectively.

Takeaways. Over the two periods analyzed, the funds' buy process unquestionably changed. Most noticeable are the shifts from purchasing stocks with relatively low levels of one-year return to much higher levels (tenth percentile up to fiftieth percentile) and the purchase of stocks with significantly lower levels of one-year sales (top quintile to the second quintile). The earlier buys reflected stocks with improving fundamentals but which may not yet have been recognized by the market, whereas the later buys seem to forgo sales growth in exchange for higher price momentum. It's unclear whether this change was intentional or inadvertent. Changes like this can indicate a helpful refinement to an already successful buy process or unintended inconsistency and potential risky future results.

The buy process for a carefully screened fund is presented in figure 8.4. The location of the range varies across attributes. The distance within the range (i.e., highest to lowest value) is fairly tight for all attributes (i.e., spanning 30% and 50%). The average attribute levels for winners and losers are very close to each other across the four attributes (cash-flow yield, operating margin, long-term debt-to-equity, and one-year return). This fund clearly is targeting stocks with a specific attribute signature. There does not appear to be a discernible difference in attribute values regarding winning and losing buys.

Takeaways. This buy process is very focused. New buys tend to come from relatively tight ranges of each attribute. The average attribute values for winners and losers are very close to each other. Such a buy process is likely to reflect consistency over time, which can be confirmed with two or three consecutive multiyear analyses. What's unknown at this time is just what level of excess return is generated from this buy process. Investigating the

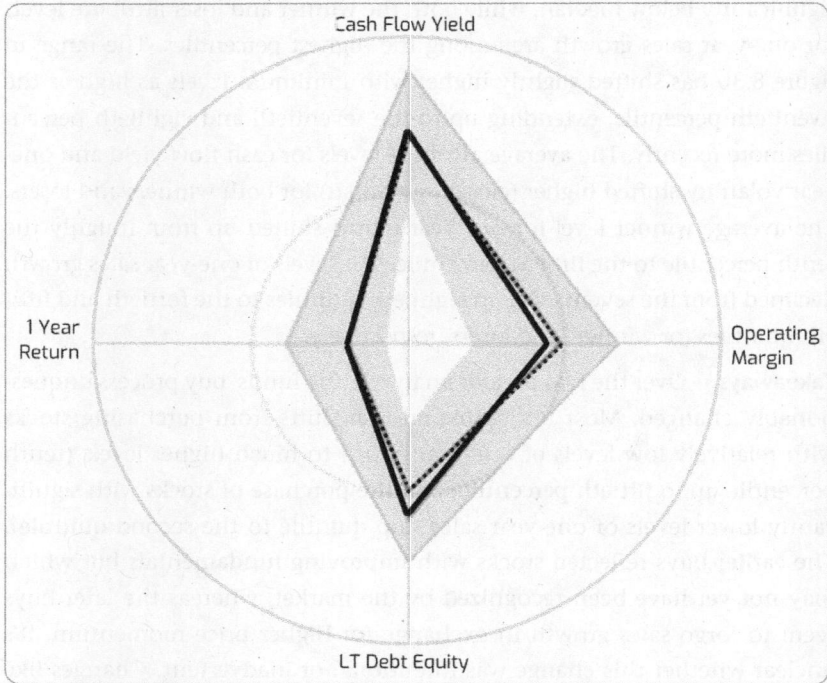

Figure 8.4
Highly targeted.

information advantage and buy skill for this fund can provide useful information about the alpha generation from new buys.

Context analysis supports understanding how the buy process is applied within individual sectors. It involves investigating attributes one at a time, across all sectors. Figure 8.5 illustrates this type of context analysis using five-year EPS growth as the attribute. It can be seen that the range of this attribute varies a good bit across the sectors. The range levels for consumer durables extend from the first percentile to the ninetieth percentile. In contrast, the range for communications services extends just 10% from the fiftieth percentile to the sixtieth percentile. Differences in average attribute levels associated with winners and losers vary as well. Within financials, the average winner attribute level is the seventieth percentile while the average for the losers is in the fortieth percentile. Both winners and losers within the utilities sector, however, have an average attribute level at

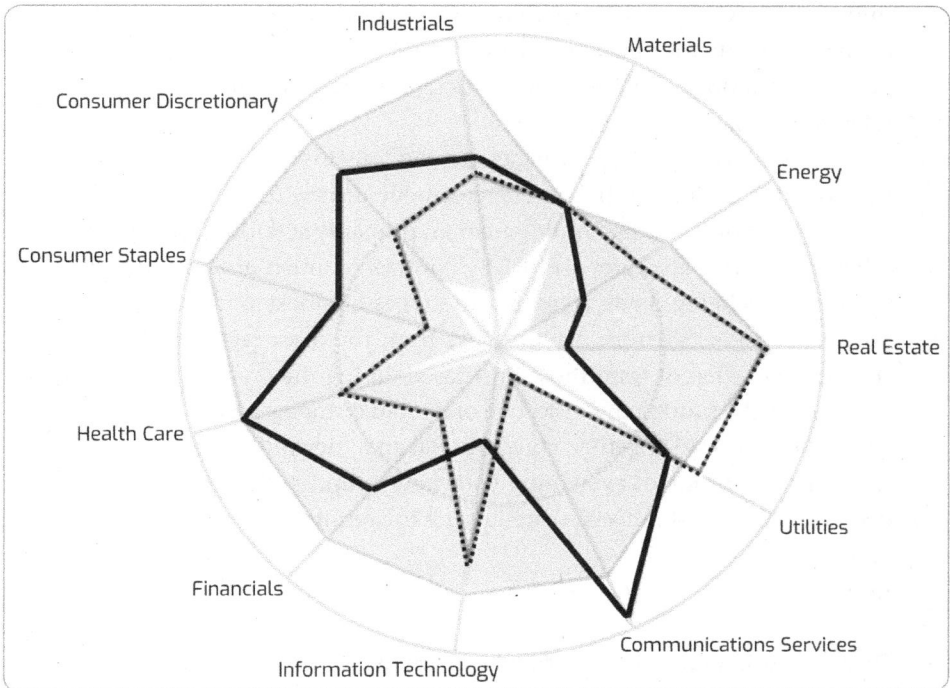

Figure 8.5
Attributes by sector.

the seventieth percentile. Dissimilarities in range and winner/loser averages may be due to different factors being more or less important across sectors or the result of differences in the judgment and processes of the research analysts covering the sectors.

Takeaways. Granular investigations like the one above are often helpful, especially when a fund's results are inconsistent or have recently fallen off. Sector investigations also help the capital allocator discern how the fund's stated buy process is playing out across the entire research team.

Actions Versus Ownership

Context analysis examines the financial characteristics common among a series of buys. This type of analysis focuses on what the typical new buy looks like at the moment of its initial purchase (i.e., it is action-based information). Conventional analytics such as attribution analysis and style analysis evaluate the characteristics (or factor loading) of all positions contained in a fund (i.e., what it owns) over the analysis period. This is also referred to as *holdings-based analysis.*

Holdings-based analysis provides tremendous insight into why a fund performed as it did. Was the excess return due mainly to stock selection or sector allocation? Did the holdings remain primarily small cap and did they reflect the anticipated growth tilt? By contrast, context analysis describes the decisions being made regarding the types of stocks purchased. It can answer questions such as: Are the buys from the most recent three years the same or different from those purchased during the previous three-year period? Are the fund's buys reflective of its stated strategy, style, and intent, or are they drifting? Together, conventional analytics and the newer analytics do a superior job of explaining both how a fund performed and which decisions (skills and processes) are driving the results.

Conclusion

Finding out if a fund outperformed recently is relatively easy. Ascertaining whether it is more or less likely to continue outperforming is the real challenge. Continued excess results require both well-honed expert judgment and highly calibrated investment processes. The latter are generally recognized as essential to delivering consistent results.

Consistently strong buys make it easier for a fund to beat its benchmark, all other things being equal. Therefore, understanding a fund's actual buy process is critical in assessing its likelihood of future outperformance. Yet very little is currently understood about the buy process. For the most part, capital allocators are limited to marketing materials and manager-provided anecdotes when attempting to assess a fund's buy process. This level of information cannot substantiate if a process exists, what types of stocks it targets, or what aspects of the buy process tend to identify winning stocks.

Context analysis is one method for describing a buy process. It uses as its input detailed contextual information about the stocks purchased by a fund. These contextual data include the date of each new buy, its sector, and the sector relative levels for a number of financial attributes that describe the stock. This information can then be plotted to provide a visualization, known as a context analysis, of the type of stocks the fund is buying.

Context analysis does more than describe the typical stock a fund is purchasing. It also indicates which financial attributes and the levels of each distinguish winning buys from losing buys. Context analysis is also used to assess the consistency of the buy process over time and across sectors. It offers tremendous insight into the buy decisions being made and their efficacy.

Context analysis enhances the assessment of a fund and its go-forward potential. Identifying a fund with a strong one-, three-, and five-year return history is exciting. Knowing that its buy process is aligned with its stated strategy, that it is regularly identifying alpha generating stocks to purchase, and that it is being applied consistently over time represents a new and deeper level of fund assessment. One that can help capital allocators make more informed and better choices.

9   To Sell or Not to Sell

One of the oldest sayings on Wall Street is "Let your winners run and cut your losers." It's easy to make a mistake and do the opposite, pulling out the flowers and watering the weeds.

—Peter Lynch

Selling can make or break fund results. Effective selling captures the alpha available from strong positions and limits the erosion of returns from weak positions. On the other hand, ineffective selling results in alpha loss when strong positions are sold prematurely and weak positions are allowed to remain in the fund far too long. Achieving the Goldilocks approach to selling—not too soon and not too late—requires skill. It's the kind of skill that is not easily acquired or readily observable. Great selling is both valuable and rare.

Defining a Good Sell

Not much is known about selling. A quick internet search makes clear that when the term *strategy* is applied to equity management, it invariably refers to buying, not selling. When it is mentioned, the act of selling is described as a discipline, which makes it sound like a humdrum activity in comparison to buying. Considerable academic research and practitioner effort has gone into studying and improving stock selection or buying. In contrast, there are very few academic papers or helpful practical guides focused on selling. Asset managers' descriptions of their selling practices tend to have a familiar set of objectives, such as "We sell when stocks hit their target prices." "We sell once a stock realizes its thesis." "We will sell opportunistically to fund a new buy." "We sell when a stock's fundamentals decline or reverse." Reasonable as these statements are, it is unclear if they actually shape selling processes or if applying them leads to effective sell decisions.

There is no generally accepted definition of what constitutes a good sell. When capital allocators and fund managers are pressed for a definition, out will come the old trope: A good sell is one in which the price of a stock goes down after it is sold. This dynamic is easy to mentally construct. It also has great intuitive appeal. This decision and outcome can represent a good sell. It can also describe a poor sell. That's right—selling a stock whose price either has peaked or begins to decline can be an ineffective sell. How is this possible? The answer is that it's relative.

Consider a fund that sells position XYZ. If subsequent to this sell the price of XYZ goes down by 10% over the following twelve months, this seems like a fairly good decision. And it is a good decision if . . . the only position that could have been sold is XYZ. If, on the other hand, the same fund held a number of weaker positions whose price dropped by 30% or more over the same period, then the sell of XYZ doesn't seem so smart. Position XYZ actually outperformed the more substantial losers that were not sold. From a fund return perspective, selling one of the even weaker positions and holding on to position XYZ would have produced a better outcome.

Consequently, there must be more to a good sell than simply liquidating a position whose price then declines. Here's a proposed definition that highlights what effective selling looks like:

Definition: A good or effective sell is one where the go-forward expected return for the position sold is below the likely go-forward return for the fund in aggregate.

In other words, the manager should sell positions likely to drag down the fund's average returns (selling the most substantial losers first) and hold on to positions likely to lift up the fund's average returns (holding on to the strongest performers the longest), all other things being equal.[1] The idea is to use selling as a means of regularly enhancing the average return of the fund. This definition emphasizes that skilled selling requires knowing when to sell as well as when to hold on to a position. It encapsulates that effective selling includes capturing the full alpha from strong buys; quickly eliminating stocks that should not have been purchased in the first place; holding on to great stocks whose price is temporarily down; and pushing out positions that have gotten tired. A deeper look into when to sell and when not to sell is provided in the next section.

Four Types of Sell Decisions

Knowing when to sell and when not to sell is important. Getting these decisions right, however, is not easy. The fund's information advantage provides useful information that can help guide sell decisions (see chapter 4). As a practical matter, effective selling requires that the manager is skilled in evaluating positions across four distinct states: younger winners, younger losers, older winners, and older losers. *Younger* and *older* refer to positions whose ages on a particular day are less than or greater than the fund's median age across all of its holdings on that same day.[2] *Winner* and *loser* denote whether, on a particular day, the position has an unrealized gain or loss.[3]

Applying the proposed sell rule across these four position states requires tremendous judgment. Some of the regularly confronted choices look like these:

- Younger winners might be approaching exhaustion and be good candidates for a sell. Alternatively, they might be in the early stages of a multimonth or multiyear run. Correctly discerning the difference can make a world of difference for fund results.

- A younger loser might be indicative of a poor buy. Alternatively, it might merely reflect a momentary negative market reaction independent of the stock's fundamentals. Knowing when to sell and when to hold is obviously important with these positions.

- An older winner may be getting tired or able to outperform for a while longer. Knowing if such a position will remain an alpha contributor or is likely to become dead money impacts how efficiently capital is recycled.

- An older loser may need to be harvested. Sometimes, however, these positions bounce back nicely and contribute meaningfully to fund returns. Choosing when to cut your losses versus hanging in there for a late game rebound is not easy.

Assessing skill within each of these four states is done with the help of counterfactual portfolios introduced in chapter 6. How this is accomplished is discussed next.

Sell Timing Analytics

Measuring how effectively positions are being harvested involves four distinct counterfactuals, one each for the four position states mentioned. The selling of younger winners is used to illustrate how the counterfactuals are constructed.

Investigating the Selling of Younger Winners

Constructing the counterfactual for assessing the selling of younger winners starts by making a copy of the actual fund history, including each position and its fund weight on each day. Each sell or trim of a younger winner is then identified and reversed through a series of adjustments. Consider position ABC, which was sold when its age was eighteen months on a day when the fund's median age for all positions held was twenty-two months (meaning ABC was a younger position). Additionally, position ABC reflected an unrealized gain at the time of its sell (it was a winner). Reversing this sell involves a series of four steps:

1. Position ABC would be repurchased up to its previous fund weight just prior to the sell. So, if its previous weight were 2%, then it would be reestablished back at 2%, on the day it was sold.

2. All other positions in the fund would simultaneously be trimmed by 2% of their size, which essentially provides the capital for the repurchase of position ABC.

3. Position ABC would then be sold after it had been held up to the fund's median age. For this example, position ABC would be repurchased when its age was eighteen months and then sold when its age reached twenty-two months.

4. The proceeds from the delayed sell of position ABC would then be allocated (added) to the fund positions on a pro rata basis.[4]

This same four-step process is then applied to each and every younger winner fully sold or trimmed throughout the fund's history. The counterfactual thus constructed is therefore answering the question: Would the fund have been better off if all the younger winners had not been sold but allowed to remain in the fund? At least until their ages reached the fund's median age? Once this counterfactual is completed, its return and relative return are then computed. The difference between the relative return of the actual fund and that of the counterfactual determines the fund's skill in selling younger winners. If the actual fund outperformed the counterfactual, this indicates that, in aggregate, the younger winners were sold and trimmed effectively. Conversely, if the actual fund underperformed the counterfactual, this result suggests that many younger winners were sold or trimmed prematurely. The counterfactual used in assessing the selling of younger losers is constructed exactly as the counterfactual above, except the younger winners are untouched and instead the sells and trims of younger losers are delayed.

Adjusting Older Positions

The counterfactuals for assessing the selling of older positions differ in that rather than delaying a sell, the sell of the older positions is advanced. For example, an older winner would have its sell advanced to when its age equaled the fund's median age and its proceeds would be redeployed (added) pro rata to the fund's remaining positions on that sell date.[5] This same two-step process would be applied to all older winners whether or not they had been sold in the actual portfolio. The question being asked by this counterfactual is: Would the fund have been better off if older winners had been sold sooner—at or near the fund's median age? The same two-step method is used to construct the counterfactual for assessing the management of older losers, only in this analysis the older winners are untouched and all older losers are sold as they hit the fund's median age.

The results of the counterfactuals described thus far are aggregate, considering all positions in each of the four sell timing states. Each of these four sell timing skills can be investigated more granularly, as discussed below.

Investigating Sell Timing Skills

The four sell timing results computed for a fund over a thirteen-year history are presented in figure 9.1. Three of the values are negative (gray bars) and one is neutral or zero (black bar). Selling of younger winners cost the fund −0.32% annually while the selling of younger losers had a zero or neutral impact. The selling of older winners and older losers impacted the fund by −0.66% and −0.52%, respectively. While none of the individual values is substantially negative the overall result is that the fund's sell skill is weak. A 1% to 1.5% negative sell skill represents a significant risk with regard to

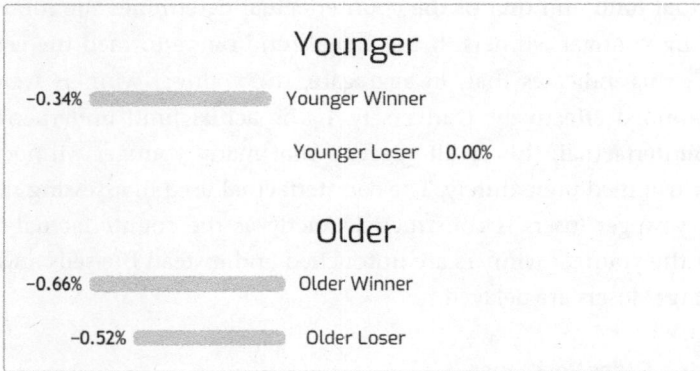

Figure 9.1
Weak selling.

future results.[6] Further erosion of these individual skills could drag an otherwise benchmark-beating fund down into underperformance.

Takeaways.   This fund's selling is challenged. Three of the sell timing skills are hurting fund results and one is neutral. Selling may present a risk concerning this fund's ability to generate excess returns going forward. A useful next step is to investigate the consistency of the fund's sell timing skills.

Sell timing values for two consecutive five-year time periods are presented in figures 9.2a and 9.2b. Two of the skills improved, one worsened, and one remained essentially the same. Younger winners remained essentially the same at a relatively low negative impact. The selling of younger losers switched from contributing positively to negatively impacting results, declining by −0.78%. The selling of older winners became less of a drag on results, improving by 2.41%. The selling of older losers also became less negative, improving by 1.54%. This is good news in that while the longer-term results above were not so favorable, it appears that the selling of older positions has improved significantly in recent years. While the trend for younger losers is not favorable, the results for the most recent five years were only modestly negative.

Takeaways.   At first glance, the sell timing results across all thirteen years were very concerning. When investigated across two five-year periods, the results appear less so. One of the skills has remained essentially the same (neutral), two skills have improved substantially, and one has declined by 0.78%, shifting from positive to negative—although its most recent results

(a)

(b)

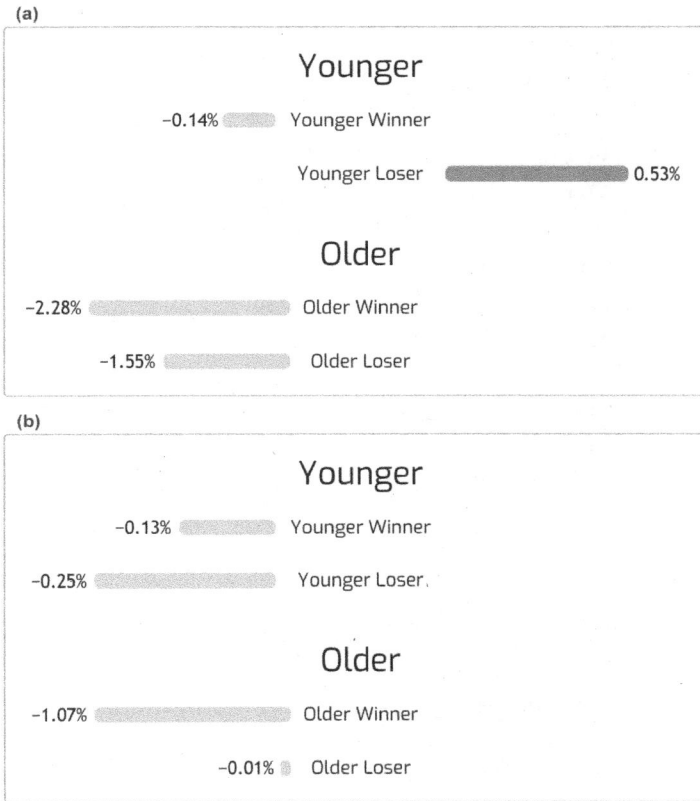

Figure 9.2
Investigating consistency.

are not alarming, at −0.25%. The sell timing results suggest that this fund's selling risk may not be as great as initially perceived. Further investigation might include a more granular look at each of the four sell timing skills.

A more in-depth investigation into the selling of older winners is presented in figure 9.3. This plot contains three distinct analytic results: thirteen years of annual values (far left), five three-year consecutive values (top right), and five distinct look-back analyses (bottom right).

The annual values for selling older winners are negative in nine of the thirteen years analyzed. The smallest negative value was −0.40% (2018) and the largest was −2.97% (2016), with many at or larger than −1%. The largest positive value is 2.55% (2011) and the smallest is 0.01% (2022). The results

One Year

	2010	1.46%
	2011	2.55%
-0.97%	2012	
-1.56%	2013	
-2.93%	2014	
	2015	0.90%
-2.97%	2016	
-0.58%	2017	
-0.40%	2018	
	2019	0.21%
	2020	0.56%
-2.39%	2021	
-0.01%	2022	

Three Year

	2010–2011	1.46%
-2.93%	2012–2014	
-0.97%	2015–2017	
-0.02%	2018–2020	
	2021–2023	0.02%

Trailing

-0.32%	Month: 02/24–02/24	
-1.12%	3 Month: 12/23–02/24	
	One Year: 03/23–02/24	0.16%
-0.03%	Three Year: 02/21–02/24	
-0.03%	Five Year: 03/19–02/24	

Figure 9.3
Granular investigation into older winners.

for the three-year averages were negative in three of the five periods. The results started out positive in the earliest period, then turned negative for the subsequent three periods, and ended up positive in the final period. The trend from the second period onward is encouraging, as the results are less and less negative and then positive. The results for the various look-back periods are less encouraging. They are negative in three of the five periods. The two most current periods of one month and three months are both negative, and the one-year value is barely positive at 0.16%. All in all, the fund's selling of older winners is challenged with no clear evidence that it is getting better.

Takeaways. The selling of older winners has been and continues to be a problem for the fund. The annual results are volatile and mostly negative. The consecutive three-year results suggested some hope that this skill might be getting better. This hope is mostly dashed as the various look-back results make clear that the selling of older winners is again negative over the most recent month, three months, and the full twelve months. Concerning this particular fund, the skill in selling older winners presents clear risks and little evidence of alpha potential.

Some funds are troubled more with their management of younger positions. The sell timing results for one such fund are presented in figure 9.4. The selling of both younger winners and younger losers is negatively impacting results at –0.83% and –0.73%, respectively. This fund is doing an excellent job in selling older winners which are adding 3.22% annually. The fund's selling of older losers is also positive at 0.49%. Ineffective selling of younger positions frequently stems from process flaws, behavioral tendencies, or both. Process issues with younger winners can result from target prices that are too low. The stocks purchased approach the targets quickly, and the process is to trim or sell as this happens. With losers, the process flaw might involve a trigger that recommends selling if the current price is sufficiently down from the initial purchase price. Behaviorally, the premature selling of younger winners relates to risk aversion or the fear that the market may take back the unrealized gain. A different behavioral tendency, known as the *aversion of pain*, can promote the premature selling of younger losers (which then frequently bounce back). The underlying motivation here is that if a stock goes down not long after being purchased, the unconscious might be suggesting: "If you think you feel badly now, imagine how you'll feel if this stock goes down even further." What's clear with this fund is that the mishandling of both younger winners and losers is dragging down returns materially.

Takeaways.   The selling of younger winners and younger losers has negatively impacted this fund by as much as –1.5% annually. This amount of

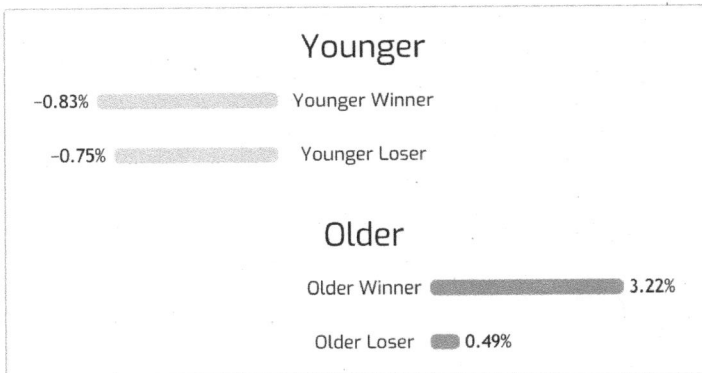

Younger		
–0.83%	Younger Winner	
–0.75%	Younger Loser	

Older		
	Older Winner	3.22%
	Older Loser	0.49%

Figure 9.4
Challenged by younger positions.

lost return can easily be the difference between first quartile and fourth quartile results for many styles. Further investigations, such as those presented in the prior example, can aid in better understanding these skills. More granular investigations can help in assessing if the selling of younger positions represents a likely risk to future results.

Conclusion

Selling is a critical skill for consistently achieving excess returns. Yet little is known about selling. It receives far less attention than does buying within academic and practitioner journals. One reflection of the paucity of insight into selling is the fact that the industry is unclear about what constitutes a good sell. It is proposed above that an effective sell decision is one where the fund's go-forward returns are enhanced as a result of the position liquidated. This definition supports quantifying if sells are either too early or too late.

The investigations presented illustrate how sell timing analyses facilitate a more rigorous understanding of a fund's sell skills. Specifically, the analyses enable the assessment of whether sell skills represent future sources of risk or alpha. This information can, in turn, support more informed fund analyses, which can lead to stronger equity allocations.

10   The Ins and Outs of Adds and Trims

Mystical additions and subtractions always come out the way you want.
—Umberto Eco

Adds and trims are the actions most frequently engaged in by fund managers. Buys and sells occur only once each as they bookend the ownership of a position. Between these start and end points, however, most positions receive numerous sizing adjustments. There are a number of reasons to build up or scale back a position's size. Attempting to capture incremental alpha is high up on this list. Whether these trades typically generate the intended outcomes is questionable. Adds and trims certainly are beneficial for some funds. For the majority, however, they reduce rather than increase excess returns. These interim trades, therefore, should not be assumed to be alpha generating or even neutral in their affects.

Is Interim Trading Necessary?

The short answer is of course. Adds and trims are important elements of overall fund management in several regards. They facilitate rebalancing that maintains position weights in line with the fund's construction rules, overall risk parameters, and seeking of excess returns. They support the fund's accommodation of inflows and outflows. Trims are used at times to fund or partially fund a new stock purchase. Adds are often used to put capital to work quickly after a position is sold. But what about those adds and trims (specifically, meaningful changes in position weights) whose purpose is to capture incremental alpha? Are these types of interim trades generally helpful? Are they a good use of the funds' capital? Do they maximize the investment potential available from the manager's intellect, energy, and time? Or might the manager's focus be better spent identifying a strong new stock to purchase or deciding which of the current holdings needs to be liquidated? These are tough questions to answer. Yet they are important. Generating fund level excess returns is challenging enough. Against this reality, engaging heavily in activities that produce a neutral or negative impact seems foolhardy at best.

Which is not to say that managers are unable to generate incremental alpha with their adds and trims. Some managers do just that. Of course, the fraction of managers that successfully execute adds and trims is far less than the number who believe they are doing so.[1] Naturally, a persistent drag on returns from adds and trims increases a fund's riskiness. Which is why quantifying the impacts of adds and trims should be a routine part of fund assessment.

Sorting Through Adds and Trims

In the context of this discussion, *adds* and *trims* refer to actions and not simply buying and selling shares. An action is the change in a position's weight, from one day to the next, that cannot be explained by price movements alone. Therefore, actions indicate changes in the allocation of a fund's capital or a shift in its bets (as described in chapter 5). More often than not, meaningful changes in position weights tend to represent alpha seeking decisions.[2] These actions are readily identified within a fund's history, and their impacts can be quantified with the use of counterfactual portfolios. In the following discussion, adds are used to illustrate conceptually how interim trading is quantified.

Constructing the Counterfactual

The counterfactual used to assess adds is similar to those described in earlier chapters. It begins with a copy of the actual fund history. From there all adds are identified and reversed. Reversal is accomplished with the now familiar two-step adjustment process described in chapters 6 and 7. Consider a fund whose first add identified in the history was applied to position KLM on May 10, 2023. In the counterfactual, this add would be reversed on the same day by selling an amount of KLM that is equal to the size of the add. Essentially the position weight of KLM would be lowered back to its pre-add level. Simultaneously, the proceeds from this sale would be reallocated to all other positions then in the fund on a pro rata basis. These same two steps of sale and reallocation would be repeated for all subsequent adds for KLM and other positions. When completed, the counterfactual would include every decision that is reflected in the actual fund, except none of the adds would have occurred. The returns and relative returns for this counterfactual are then computed.

The impact of the adds is computed by comparing the relative return of the actual fund to the relative return of the counterfactual portfolio. If the difference is positive, then, on average, the adds helped. If the difference is negative, then the adds did more harm than good. Trims are assessed using essentially the same two-step process in reverse. Each trim identified is nullified by building the position back up to its pre-trim weight. The weight added back is funded by selling (trimming) a pro rata share of all other positions in the fund on the same day. The returns and relative returns are then computed for the counterfactual. If the difference in results between the actual fund and the counterfactual is positive, this indicates that the trims were helpful, and if the difference is negative, this indicates the trims were unhelpful.

Further segmenting adds and trims to consider positions with either unrealized gains (winners) or unrealized losses (losers) supports a more granular investigation into the add and trim skills. This four-quadrant approach (adds to winners, adds to losers, trims to winners, trims to losers) is explored in the following analyses.

Adding, Trimming, Winning, Losing

The range of impacts that can be delivered by adds and trims are considered in this section. The results presented are based on actual actively managed equity funds.

Effective add and trim results for a fund are presented in figure 10.1. The impacts from adding to winners, adding to losers, and trimming of losers are all positive, with trimming of winners being essentially neutral. The largest individual benefit came from trimming losers at 0.44%. In aggregate adds and trims have lifted fund results in excess of 0.50% annually.[3] Success or even modest success in all four add and trim skills is rare.

Add

Add Up   0.08%

Add Down   0.39%

Trim

Trim Up   0.00%

Trim Down   0.41%

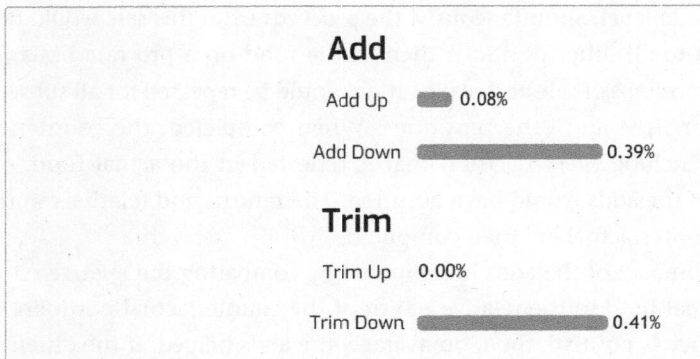

Figure 10.1
Modestly successful interim trading.

Takeaways. Positive add and trim skills, even modest ones, are a welcome result. Yet, with only the trimming of losers approaching a benefit of 0.50%, it seems wise to confirm the consistency of these results. Modest skills, should they prove to be volatile, can quickly change from sources of incremental alpha to sources of risk. The uncovering of such volatility can substantially alter the assessment of a fund's desirability.

Figure 10.2 presents the successful add and trim results for a fund. Positive relative returns are being captured from all four skills, which is impressive. The single largest contributor to these results comes from trimming winners at 0.90% per year. Results like this are representative of the top quintile of add and trim skills for active equity managers.[4]

Takeaways. This fund is capturing significant incremental returns from adds and trims across the board. Strong interim trading like this is uncommon. Deeper analysis to understand the persistence of these skills can aid in assessing their repeatability going forward.

Trims and adds can feel right at the moment they are executed only to later generate severely negative impacts, as shown in figure 10.3. All four add and trim skills for this fund are substantially negative. The greatest losses came from adds to winners, which generated −1.86% of incremental alpha annually. The combined effects of adds and trims is an enormous drag on annual results for this fund.

Takeaways. Few funds can suffer the negative results from interim trading shown above and still deliver positive excess returns. Funds with negative

add and trim skills are usually unaware of the damage such trades are causing. Reversing past interim trading results from highly negative values to
neutral alone would provide a marked improvement for this fund. Historic
skills like these could, in the right situation, provide the backdrop for a
rebound investment opportunity. A fund with such a past that can provide credible assurance that their past losses from interim trading were now
under control might well be worth a fresh look.

Value funds often exhibit a clear pattern of adding to losers while trimming winners. Done with excess enthusiasm, this behavior results in a fund

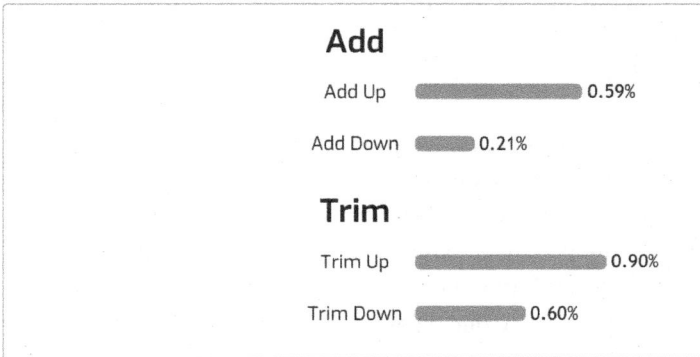

Figure 10.2
Strong add and trim skills.

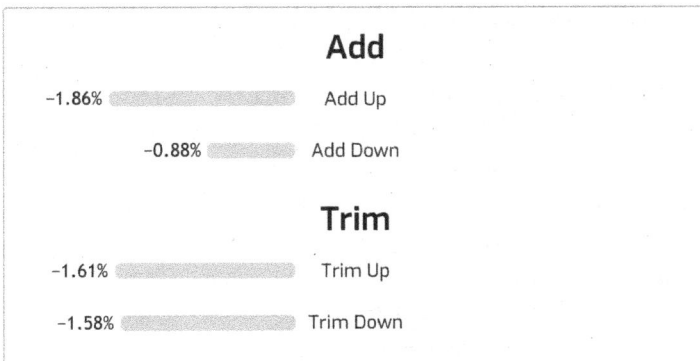

Figure 10.3
Trading away alpha.

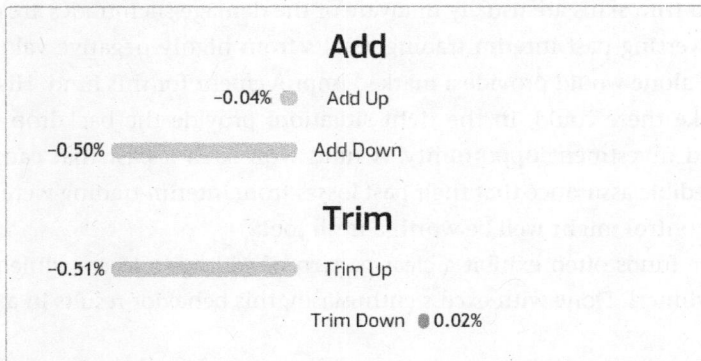

Add

-0.04% Add Up

-0.50% Add Down

Trim

-0.51% Trim Up

Trim Down 0.02%

Figure 10.4
The other value trap.

being overinvested in underperforming positions and underinvested in its higher performers. The outcomes from this type of trading bias can range from merely dampening fund results all the way to driving the fund's returns well below its benchmark. Such could be the case shown in figure 10.04. As the numbers indicate, adds to losers are generating –0.50% relative returns while trims to winners are also reducing results by an additional 0.51%. This trading behavior seems to epitomize the notion of watering the weeds while pulling the flowers. This type of trimming and adding concentrates capital in value positions that have not begun to, or may never, perform well.

Takeaways. Value investing occasionally encounters headwinds due to market dynamics. Overfeeding losers combined with not allowing winners to run with sufficient capital can exacerbate cyclical challenges. The interim trading dynamic illustrated in this example may be, in good part, an unintended consequence of style conformity. This can lead to a value fund trimming positions that have grown out of their value characteristics while simultaneously plowing these sale proceeds back into positions with more obvious value qualities. This example raises the question of style adherence. Should value funds both buy and hold only value stocks, or should they buy value stocks and then have the freedom to hold them as they grow and generate excess returns for the fund? The latter approach might enable value funds to deliver strong results more regularly. Such a change would place the value criteria directly on the buying and allow the fund's overall holdings to reflect less of a value characteristic or even become slightly growthy.

Aggregate interim trading skills that deliver both positive and consistent results are great finds. Observing how these skills manifest themselves by examining position-level decisions can provide further insight into how alpha is being generated or lost. The adds and trims used in managing an individual position are presented in figure 10.5.[5]

Adds and trims are indicated by the elongated bubble shapes. The darker shaded bubbles are adds and the lighter shaded bubbles are trims. The y-axis on the left denotes the position's returns. The position's weight is indicated by the y-axis on the right. Time is demarcated by the x-axis. The position shown was purchased in 2014 at the beginning of a multiyear run-up in price. The manager trimmed the position in 2015, which in retrospect appears to be ill-timed since the price went up afterward. Two effective adds were then made in 2019 as the position's price was climbing. The manager then trimmed the position at a high point just ahead of a significant price

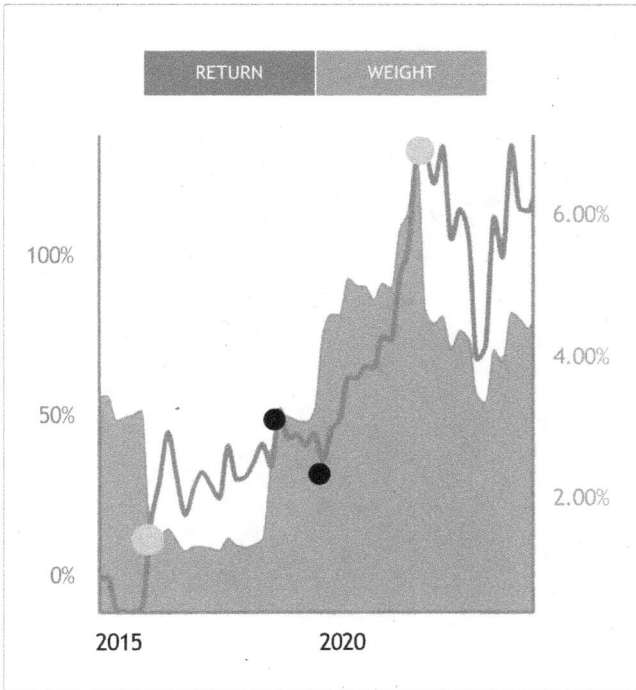

Figure 10.5
Visualizing adds and trims.

reversal. The position was untouched through the remainder of the analysis timeframe. This position experienced a mixed set of add and trim decisions that were largely effective.

Takeaways. Knowing that a manager is skilled at adds and trims in aggregate is valuable information. Additionally, observing how adds and trims are applied to individual positions can enrich the understanding and assessment of these skills. Plots like those in figure 10.5 make it possible to see that the majority of add and trim decisions either helped or hurt. This information can lead to more effective fund assessment and stronger equity allocations.

Adds on the way down can reflect the manager's taking advantage of a temporary price dip—essentially enabling the additional purchase of a great stock at a bargain price. Adds on a price dip can also reflect a miscalculation or even desperation on the part of the manager.[6] The alpha erosion that can result from adds to the wrong position is illustrated in figure 10.6.

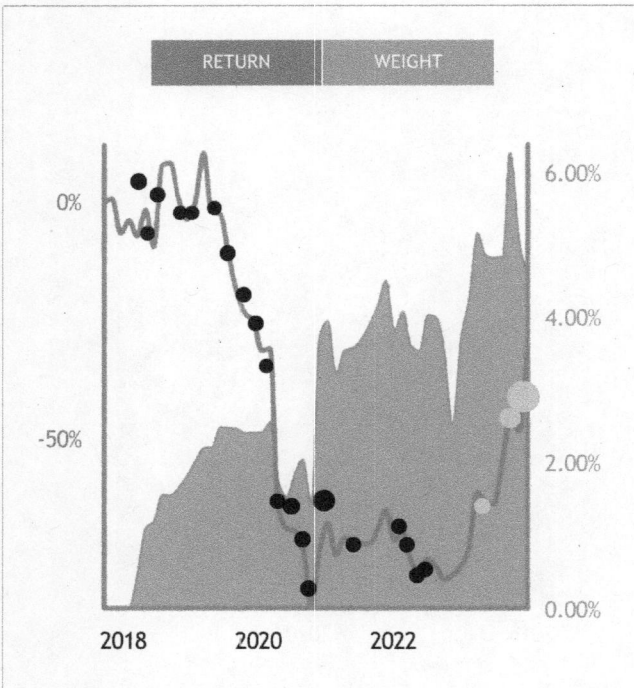

Figure 10.6
Adding on the way down, and down, and down.

This stock was purchased in 2018. The stock took a mild dip in price shortly after purchase, during which the manager made several adds. Then, beginning in 2019, the stock began a protracted decline stretching through 2022, during which its price dropped approximately 80%. Several more adds were made during this timeframe. Roughly 7.5% of the fund's total capital was eventually poured into this position (i.e., initial sizing plus all adds). Yet, its portfolio weight remained below 4.5%. This indicates that while additional capital was invested, a good bit of it was lost. The stock's price began to rebound in 2023, after five years of ownership, at which point the manager began to trim the position. Despite several more trims on the way up, the position was being held at a sizable loss at the conclusion of this analysis period.

Takeaways. Sometimes a price dip suggests a buying opportunity. At other times it signals a weak position that should be sold. Data-driven illustrations like the one above can help strengthen the fund assessment process and enrich allocator-manager discussions.

Conclusion

Adds and trims are common actions applied to fund positions. Their intent often is to capture incremental alpha. This objective is sometimes realized, but less frequently than believed.

Funds need to adjust the sizes of positions they own for reasons other than capturing incremental returns. Adds and trims to accommodate inflows and outflows, manage overall risk profile, and adherence to portfolio construction and style constraints are among the reasons. Analyzing alpha seeking decisions versus those executed for other reasons provides clear feedback on active management. The use of actions distinguishes alpha seeking efforts from other activities. The impacts of these actions can be quantified with the use of counterfactual portfolios.

The examples presented reflect the widely divergent outcomes generated by adds and trims. Interim trading can be the source of welcome incremental alpha or can subject a fund to unwanted risk. Consequently, gaining greater knowledge about the impacts of adds and trims enables capital allocators to make more informed and ultimately more effective investment decisions.

11   Know When to Fold 'Em

People, it turns out, are not that averse to risk. For many reasons, they are not opposed to risk, but they are opposed to losing and the possibility of loss plays a very significant part in their decisions.

—Daniel Kahneman

Realizing a loss is painful. And the bigger the loss, the greater the pain experienced. So much so that some funds are more inclined to hold on to positions with substantial unrealized losses rather than sell them and move on. If this reluctance occurs periodically, its impact may be relatively benign. On the other hand, when this type of behavior is repeated regularly, the results can be very damaging.

Loss Aversion

Individuals will go to great lengths to avoid realizing a loss. This cognitive frailty was observed by the behavioral finance pioneers Daniel Kahneman and Amos Tversky.[1] They termed this tendency *loss aversion*. It's motivated by the desire to sidestep the negative feelings that can accompany selling at a loss—feelings that, for some, may unconsciously suggest thoughts like "If this position is sold at a loss, then maybe I'm a bit of a loser as well?" To the extent these thoughts are present, it is highly understandable why individuals would avoid such harsh interior self-admonishment.

Sorting out whether or not to liquidate a substantial loser (i.e., significant unrealized loss) is challenging and laden with risks. If a substantial loser should rebound, this turnabout would represent a financial recovery for the fund. It might also provide an (unconscious) psychic redemption for the manager, as in "That stock bounced back and now I'm off the hook." Absent the desired rebound, however, the same position represents the unproductive deployment of precious capital. Worse, the price of this position might continue its downward trajectory, compounding its negative impact on fund results. It has been suggested that for some, just contemplating substantial losers can evoke sufficient psychic pain so as to make them too difficult to review.

Over the past five decades numerous studies have investigated and confirmed this human tendency to sidestep emotional pain by holding on to losers. Neuroscience researcher Huixin Tan and colleagues were able to link loss aversion to identifiable emotional distress.[2] Using functional magnetic resonance imaging, the team showed that financial losses stimulate the same pain center in the brain as do losses in social status. And if you've ever committed an egregious social faux pas (or witnessed someone doing so), then you understand the painful effects of public humiliation. The anguish that can accompany an embarrassing comment or display is intense and can leave an indelible imprint on the perpetrator's psyche. Financial losses, it seems, can deliver comparable psychic injuries.

The relatively new discipline of emotional finance provides additional insight into the motivational forces behind loss aversion. Formulated by Richard Taffler and David Tuckett, emotional finance is based on the Freudian concept that many human actions are motivated by the desire to either seek pleasure or avoid pain.[3] When considered within this framework, holding on to substantial losers that generally don't rebound is an obvious effort to avoid pain. Notwithstanding the bravado from some fund managers, which sounds something like "We make all our decisions completely by the numbers, with no emotional baggage," fund managers are unquestionably emotional beings. Their judgment and discipline are constantly being tested by financial-related stressors, such as unrealized gains and losses, market volatility, being above or below benchmark results, rising or lowering in peer group ranking, and capital flows. Each stressor can spark emotions that may override analytic decision-making and lead to choices that are emotionally satisfying in the near term but whose outcomes are financially ruinous.

Behavioral finance, neuroscience, and emotional finance provide a strong intellectual foundation for understanding why dealing with losses can be problematic. Assessing the likely presence or absence of loss aversion, therefore, seems like a valuable adjunct to assessing the riskiness of a fund.

The Management of Substantial Losers

Loss aversion exists within equity management, and its impacts can deplete fund returns. This section looks at how to identify the presence of loss aversion and quantify its impact. Doing so involves use of the now familiar counterfactual portfolio to suss out if a fund would have been better off selling its substantial losers than allowing them to remain.

Constructing the Counterfactual

Once again, the analysis begins with a copy of the actual fund history. Next, a level of unrealized loss level is chosen as a threshold or trip wire, the idea being that any position whose unrealized loss equals or exceeds the threshold will be sold in the counterfactual. A common loss level for this purpose is 20%. All positions in the history with unrealized losses equal to or greater than the threshold are then identified, along with the day each first hits the threshold (the *threshold date*). These positions are then sold on the threshold date, and their proceeds are redeployed pro rata across all other positions in the fund.

Let's consider how an individual substantial loser is adjusted in constructing this type of counterfactual. Position ABC is the first substantial loser encountered in a fund's history. It experienced an unrealized loss of greater than 20% on June 30, 2021 (i.e., the threshold date). In the actual fund, this position was held through December 31, 2024. In the counterfactual portfolio, position ABC is sold on its threshold date. This has the effect of advancing the liquidation of this position by forty-two months. Simultaneously, the sale proceeds from position ABC are reinvested pro rata across all other positions in the fund. This same two-step adjustment is then repeated for all other substantial losers identified throughout the entire fund history. Upon completion, the counterfactual created reflects all of the managers' actual decisions with the exception that each position that experienced a 20% or more loss would have been eliminated on the day its loss first hit the threshold. The returns and relative returns of this counterfactual are then computed.

The skill in managing substantial losers is calculated as the difference in relative returns between the actual fund and the counterfactual.[4] A positive difference indicates that the substantial losers were managed effectively in aggregate (i.e., selling them sooner did not improve results). A negative result highlights that the fund would have been better off had some or many of the substantial losers been sold sooner (i.e., many did not bounce back).

Additional insights into this skill are available from more granular investigations. For starters, it is useful to test multiple loss thresholds such as down 20%, 30%, and 40% to learn how sensitive the results are to the loss threshold chosen. The analysis can be also performed by sector and by financial attribute to learn if there are types of substantial losers more or less likely to be held too long. And, of course, each analysis can be performed over multiple consecutive periods to investigate persistence. The following discussion illustrates how a deeper understanding of this skill may be acquired.

When to Harvest, When to Let Grow

Quantifying how effectively substantial losers are being managed provides great insight into future outperformance as well as a valuable complement to traditional risk metrics. The following examples demonstrate the value derived from a thorough investigation of this skill.

The impact from poor management of substantial losers within an actual fund are presented in figure 11.1. All three results are negative, indicating that the simulated results of the counterfactual portfolios outperformed the actual fund. Not selling positions as they hit the 20% loss threshold lowered fund results by 1.22%. Not selling positions as they reached the 30% and then 40% thresholds reduced fund results by 0.13% and 0.06%, respectively. What's interesting is that positions sold at the lower threshold (down 20%) had a larger negative impact while those sold at the higher thresholds (deeper losses) had a smaller negative impact. Several factors may be contributing to this set of results. One potential explanation is

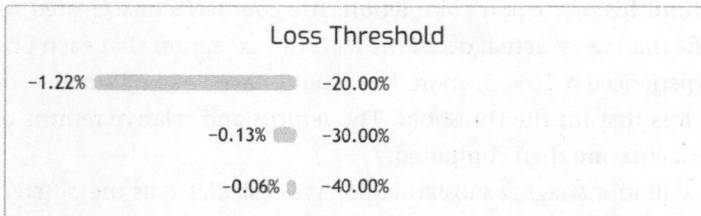

Figure 11.1
Lingering losers.

that there were more positions and/or more capital invested in those positions that experienced losses between 20% and less than 30% versus higher loss levels. Another possibility is that the positions down 20% or so were allowed to linger in the fund while those down 30% and more were sold more effectively.

Discussions with managers regarding substantial losers is often focused on the most egregious current losers (i.e., positions that are down significantly and/or heavily weighted). This type of review typically involves a discussion of why the manager thinks the positions have underperformed and how each position is now being managed. It is not at all unimaginable that for many funds the selling of the deepest losers may be motivated, at least in part, to avoid or limit such interrogations. Ironically, as this example demonstrates, there may be more harm done to a fund from its lesser losers than those with the most substantial losses. These results underscore both the risks that substantial losers can pose to fund outcomes and the challenges faced in sussing out their impacts using current metrics and practices.

Takeaways.   Those positions that have experienced a somewhat moderate (20%) price drop can (as a group) have a larger negative impact on fund results than those with greater price declines, as this example so clearly demonstrates. This is one reason that the newer analytics that assess decisions and actions are such powerful complements to conventional metrics. Results like these enable the capital allocator to understand what is really helping or hurting fund results and where significant fund management risks may exist.

Persistence can be examined through analyzing discrete intervals over longer horizons. Figure 11.2 presents the results from this type of analysis across three consecutive three-year periods for a different fund. The impact from holding substantial losers is meaningfully negative for all three threshold levels in the earliest period (2015–2017). The largest adverse impact equals –0.91% for the 20% threshold. The results decrease to –0.85% at the 30% threshold and –0.66% at the 40% threshold. The results from the second period (2018–2020) are clearly different. The 20% and 30% thresholds resulted in much larger negative impacts equaling –2.31% and –1.47%, respectively. Positions down by more than 40% appear to be managed effectively in this time frame since the result is 0.01% (indicating that selling these positions would not have helped). Results for the third or latest period

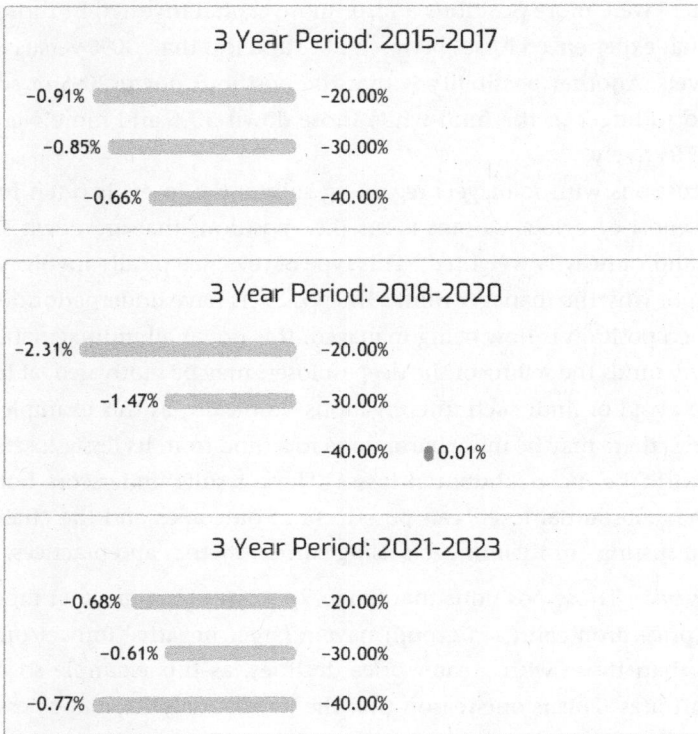

Figure 11.2
Looking for persistence.

(2021–2023) are all negative and fairly close together. The values for the 20%, 30% and 40% thresholds are –0.68%, –0.61%, and 0.77%, respectively.

It's obvious that substantial losers have detracted from this fund's results over the years analyzed. The level of negative impact did vary across the three periods studied. Substantial losers at all three thresholds were particularly costly to the fund during the second period.

Takeaways. While there is some volatility in results across the three periods studied, substantial losers were a persistent drag on fund returns throughout. In particular, positions that are down 20% and 30% are giving away well over 0.6% of incremental return annually across the full history, the results in the second period being two and three times this level. The general persistence and occasional deeply negative values indicate that this fund has a risk exposure with regard to the management of substantial losers.

Examining the management of substantial losers in relation to various financial attributes can help isolate where the selling of these positions is distinctively unproductive. The analysis performed is identical to that explained above with one refinement. Each threshold investigation includes two counterfactual portfolios, one involving only positions with relatively high attribute values and the other involving positions with relatively low attribute values. This subdivision by relative attribute values doubles the number of counterfactuals from three to six, as discussed.

Results from analyzing a fund's management of substantial losers, bifurcated by positions with relatively strong and weak balance sheets (i.e., relatively low debt-to-asset ratios and relatively high debt-to-asset ratios) are presented in figure 11.3. One group of results reflects the relatively strong balance sheet quality analyses and the other the relatively weaker balance sheet quality analyses. The results for the stronger balance sheet group are all positive, indicating that substantial losers with less debt are being sold effectively. The weaker balance sheet group tells a different story. Had these substantial losers been sold as they experienced a 20% drop in price, the fund would have captured an additional 0.73% of incremental return annually. Lesser benefits would have come from selling positions as they hit the 30% and 40% loss thresholds.

Asymmetries in results between relatively low and high attribute levels are not uncommon. Differences in results by attribute level may be due to any number of things. One possibility is a shift in market sentiment (i.e., an attribute coming into and out of favor) that is slow to be detected. Another might be the concomitant strength or shortcomings of the fund's aptitudes (e.g., fundamental research, expert judgment, decision processes) with regard to reconfirming the thesis of positions with relatively low and high levels of a financial attribute.

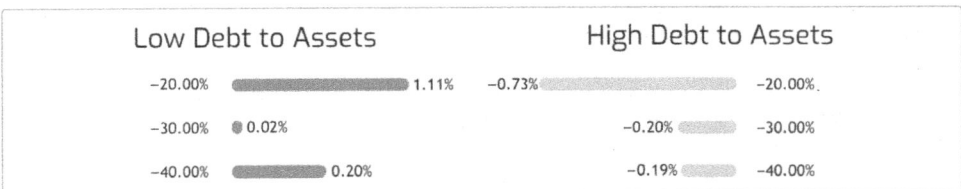

Figure 11.3
Analysis by financial attribute.

Takeaways. Analyses by attribute can deliver insights into how substantial losers of varying financial character are being managed and what their impact is on fund results. In this example, substantial losers with strong balance sheet quality are being managed well. Substantial losers with lower balance sheet quality, on the other hand, represent a headwind for the fund. Granular analyses like these can isolate pockets of weak decision-making, allowing for the more discerning assessment of fund riskiness and overall desirability.

An analysis of the management of substantial losers by sector is presented in figure 11.4. The results indicate that this fund is managing substantial losers well in some sectors, adequately in a few, and not so effectively in others. Substantial losers appear to be managed well in the Consumer Staples and Consumer Discretionary sectors, with both having positive skill measures of over 0.5% annually. The sectors where substantial losers seem to be allowed to remain in the fund for too long include Industrials and Materials, with results of –0.69% and –0.51%, respectively. These dissimilarities may be due

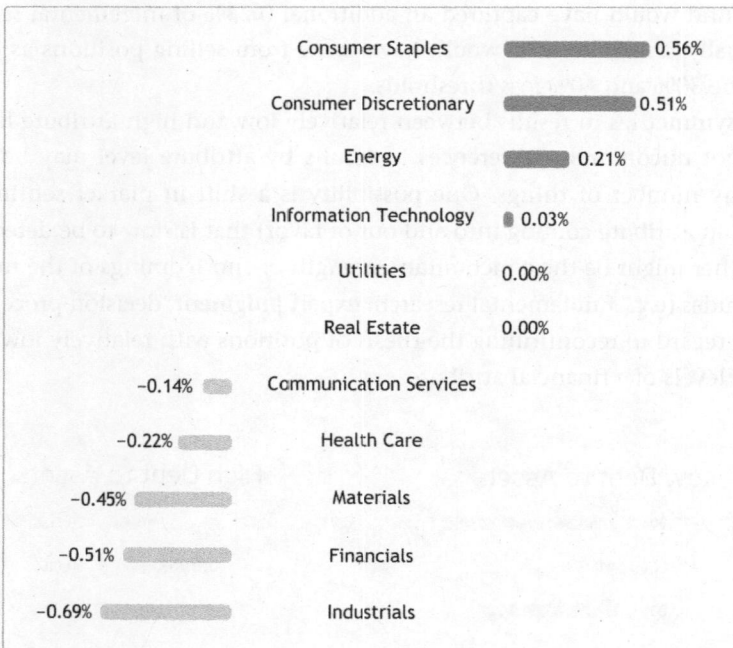

Consumer Staples	0.56%
Consumer Discretionary	0.51%
Energy	0.21%
Information Technology	0.03%
Utilities	0.00%
Real Estate	0.00%
Communication Services	–0.14%
Health Care	–0.22%
Materials	–0.45%
Financials	–0.51%
Industrials	–0.69%

Figure 11.4
Analysis by sector.

to any number of things, including differences in the skill levels of the analysts covering the sectors or dispersion of performance across sectors over the period analyzed. Large negative values in one or more sector(s) portends a greater chance of return volatility for a fund going forward.

Takeaways. Assessing any skill by sector (or global region) can be useful. It may identify a small number of problematic sectors that are accountable for the lion's share of a negative skill value. Alternatively, the analysis may confirm that the skill deficit is pervasive across sectors. The results in figure 11.4 identify two sectors where the management of substantial losers is negatively impacting results by 0.5% or more. Combining these results with the sell skill by sector and sell timing by sector can help assess whether the management of substantial losers is a likely risk for this fund going forward.

The results for a fund that is successfully managing substantial losers are presented in figure 11.5. The values for all three loss thresholds are positive. This indicates that the quicker selling of these positions would not benefit this fund. This success in managing substantial losers may be due to any of several fund management skills, such as a strong buy skill and tight buy process, which can reduce the number and severity of weak purchases, or a highly effective review process for assessing the go-forward potential of substantial losers, enabling them to be harvested efficiently. It's clear that the fund in this example is managing substantial losers well. The rigorous confirmation provided by this type of analysis can enable a fund review to swiftly and confidently refocus to other skill areas.

Industry Observation

The familiar stop-loss question came into vogue in response to the harsh experiences of most capital allocators during the 2008–2009 financial crisis.

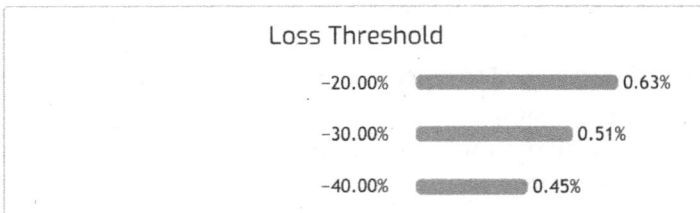

Loss Threshold

−20.00%	0.63%
−30.00%	0.51%
−40.00%	0.45%

Figure 11.5
When skill abounds.

Many equity funds held firmly to financials and other stocks during this period. Quite a few of these stocks went down substantially in price and never recovered (e.g., Lehman Brothers). Others took years to bounce back. Consequently, "what if they had implemented a stop-loss rule" became a common shorthand for wondering if a manager had adequate review processes in place. In particular, these capital allocators want to know if the funds in which they have invested are prepared to manage substantial losers more effectively today or expose them to another painful ride.

Managing substantial losers is, as reflected in the examples above, a more subtle skill than can be fully assessed from the answers to one or more stop-loss questions. Nor can the right level of insight be gained from performing a back-of-the-envelope stop-loss analysis. The newer analytics help ensure that what could be a grave risk is surfaced when this knowledge can be most useful (i.e., decision time).

Conclusion

It is generally understood that risk and return are positively correlated. Yet despite the willingness to accept risk, most individuals abhor losses. And this aversion to taking losses is found abundantly among equity fund managers as well. Academic research confirms this apparent paradox, as do observations from actual actively managed equity funds. Loss aversion is a specific manifestation of how bold intentions (taking on risk) can turn into timid behaviors (unwillingness to realize a loss). Hanging on to substantial losers that rarely rebound can have a meaningfully negative impact on fund returns. Understanding if this practice is present, and its past impact on fund results, is crucial information for capital allocators.

Asking about how current substantial losers are being managed is often employed as a due diligence probe. This helps in learning why the positions in question have underperformed and what plan is in place for managing these positions going forward. Additionally, simplistic stop-loss calculations are sometimes used to provide a bit more insight into how substantial losers are being managed.

The newer analytics can provide more rigorous and granular answers to these questions. One such approach involves the use of counterfactual portfolios. This form of analysis can provide capital allocators with a deeper understanding of how these positions have been managed and their likely riskiness going forward.

The understanding of manager skills is deepening. Differentiating a fund's ability to effectively manage all losers generally versus how well substantial losers are being managed is an important distinction that supports more informed manager assessment. Analyses like those presented in this chapter can help capital allocators in their efforts to identify who is more or less likely to generate excess returns going forward.

12 Size Really Does Matter

Our lives are defined by opportunities. Even the ones we miss.
—F. Scott Fitzgerald

Sizing can make the difference between generating excess returns or delivering ho hum results. Buying and selling skills are critically important, of course. Not building up the strongest positions in a timely manner, however, can put the alpha generating brakes on even an outstanding collection of stocks. Building up winners before their prices run up allows these outperforming positions to lift fund results handsomely. Not building them up expeditiously, however, curtails their ability to contribute significantly to fund returns. Knowing how well a fund captures the full potential of its strongest buys is, therefore, of sizable importance.

The Sizing Challenge

Capturing excess returns at the fund level requires investing more capital in the strongest positions and less in the weaker ones. Despite this obvious truism, little is known about position initial sizing. A fund might very well buy and own some of the best stocks during each market period and still struggle or fail to outperform. In these situations, the root cause is frequently the misallocation of capital. It's manifested in part by not building up, at the time of initial purchase, those buys that go on to generate significant outperformance.[1] Another expression of this misallocation is far too much capital being tied up in what ultimately prove to be poor or lackluster buys. For the most part, sizing is not given its full due in either its analytic assessment or its implementation. Sizing regimes frequently are shaped by misinformation and mislearnings, such as guesstimates based on past results, pearls of wisdom handed down from mentors to highly impressionable junior managers, unverified industry rules of thumb, educated guesses, and unconscious desires. This type of pseudoknowledge often bolsters conviction when real understanding is weak or absent. It motivates decisions that may feel right but whose outcomes are far less than desired.

Naturally, there are funds that do size positions well. They get plenty of capital behind their strongest buys. They don't overweight purchases that ultimately become laggards. And they exercise both abilities with sufficient regularity so that little opportunity is missed in capturing incremental returns from their initial sizing decisions. These funds are the exception, however. Mostly, weak or nonexistent calibration of sizing skills reigns. Building up winners is a sufficiently important skill that if it is ignored in the manager assessment process, an unidentified deficit can turn a perceived opportunity into misfortune, expectation into despair, and a hopeful allocation into a regrettable experience.

Ramping Things Up

Capturing the full potential from a great buy requires decisiveness, meaning the position must be large enough when it is outperforming to make a difference at the fund level. Consider position XYZ, whose size was 0.5% of total fund capital twelve months ago and which earned a 30% return over the intervening year, with no adds to position weight. Despite its stellar return its contribution to overall fund results was very modest due to its paltry size during the run-up.[2] In contrast, position ABC earned a return of 20% over the same period yet because its weight was 7% of fund capital at the beginning of the year, this position made a much more significant contribution to fund returns. Misalignment between position sizing and realized returns is both common and very expensive. The more frequently strong buys run up in price while sized inadequately, the greater the alpha that is being foregone (i.e., missed opportunities). Consequently, understanding a fund's effectiveness in building up new buys provides important information when assessing the return and risk characteristics of an allocation. Before delving into how the skill of initial position sizing is computed, it is useful to first review what can be learned about initial sizing from the newer analytics described in previous chapters.

Buying, Sizing, and Returns

The buy and sizing skills, together with the fund relative return, can provide some indication of how effectively positions are being built up. The buy skill describes how much excess return is available from the fund's typical new buy. Higher buy skills should result in higher fund returns, all other things being equal.[3] The sizing skill informs (to a good extent) how much of the alpha potential from new buys is actually being captured through effective sizing of positions. Relative return measures the difference between the fund's returns and those of its benchmark. In combination, these metrics provide an initial glimpse into how well winners are being sized. For example: A fund with a strong buy skill, weak sizing skill, and only modest relative returns may not be building up winners effectively. Alternatively, a fund with a modest buy skill and a strong sizing skill and which is close to or exceeding its benchmark may be doing so, in good part, by effectively building up winners before they take off. It should be kept in mind that the sizing skill combines the effect of both initial position buildup and interim trading (i.e., adds and trims). Therefore, any preliminary insights regarding the building up of winners from these metrics should be viewed as suggestive rather than conclusive. More complete descriptions of the buy and sizing skills are available in chapter 7.

The Information Advantage

This analytic describes how a fund's average new buy contributes to the fund's total returns over time. It quantifies where, across five time intervals unique to each fund, new purchases tend to generate their strongest returns relative to fund average returns. Highly positive relative contribution early on indicates that the typical buy generates a good portion of its alpha soon after purchase. Conversely, strong relative contribution far into the average holding period points out that the majority of outperformance comes in the latter stages of a fund's stock ownership (see chapter 4 for more on this topic).

The information advantage can be thought of as a profile of how and when the returns from new buys tend to be above or below the fund itself. Ideally, new buys should be brought up to full weight just as they begin to outperform.[4] When the information advantage is strongly front-loaded (i.e., winners tend to take off shortly after purchase), getting to full weight quickly can be highly beneficial. On the other hand, if the typical new buy does not begin to generate excess returns for weeks or months after purchase, then there is plenty of time to establish a full position weight. Thus, the information advantage offers a helpful guide as to how a fund should be building up its winners. Moreover, a quick glance at a fund's buy and sizing skills together with its information advantage can indicate if further investigation into sizing might be helpful. Unanswered questions can then be investigated with ramp-up analysis.

Ramp-Up Analysis

Not building up positions effectively can be costly, as has been discussed. Learning just how effectively new buys are being brought up to full weight is accomplished with the help of ramp-up analysis. The results of this analysis shed light on whether a fund's strongest buys are already being sized effectively or if a more rapid buildup of position weights would improve fund returns. Ramp-up analysis is performed using the familiar counterfactual portfolio analytic (see chapter 6).

Constructing the Counterfactual

Ramp-up analysis begins with a copy of the actual fund history. Next, all new buys with actual weights less than the fund's current full weight (*undersized buys*) are identified. New buys are given the fund's typical number of days to reach full position size before such determination is finalized. Then, beginning with the first undersized buy, its size is brought up to the fund's full weight commencing immediately after the date of initial purchase (more on commencement times below). The buildup may be accomplished in one add or multiple adds over many days, depending on the amount of stock required and the fund's liquidity tolerance. Next, a pro rata share of all other positions in the fund is sold to fund the add(s). This two-step adjustment is repeated for all undersized buys in the fund's history. The result is a counterfactual portfolio that reflects all of the managers' actual decisions with the exception that each time a new buy was undersized, it was brought up to full position weight commencing immediately.

The return and relative return of the counterfactual portfolio is then computed. The difference in relative return between the actual fund and the counterfactual measures the fund's success in building up new buys. If the difference is positive, then the ramping up is unhelpful (i.e., the fund's initial sizing is effective). If the difference is negative, this indicates that ramping up faster did help (i.e., many new buys were undersized for too long). This latter result highlights that alpha is being missed. Specifically, a good number of new buys are beginning their move up in price while not having at least a full position weight.

In practice it is useful to investigate multiple ramp-up initiation periods. In addition to ramping up commencing immediately, the start of ramping up might be delayed a few weeks or months. Multiple commencement dates for ramping up provide insight into just how sensitive alpha capture is to the timing of when undersized buys are built up. The results from multiple ramp-up commencement dates also provide additional insight into the fund's information advantage. The time intervals between ramp-up commencement dates are typically bespoke to each fund, reflecting its unique information advantage. This might involve all ramp-up commencement dates being closer to the initial buy date for a fund with a front-loaded information advantage. By contrast, using longer intervals between successive ramp-up commencement dates would be appropriate for a fund whose information advantage is more elongated or perhaps back-ended. Examples of how ramp-up analysis is used to further assess a fund's sizing skill follow.

Benefits of Ramp-Up Analysis

Adding more capital to new buys soon after purchase can be helpful or not depending on the buy skill, the information advantage, and the fund's current initial sizing practices. The analyses that follow illustrate how fund initial sizing can be investigated and the results incorporated into fund assessment.

The ramp-up results for a fund that seems to be sizing positions successfully are shown in figure 12.1. The buildup of undersized positions is

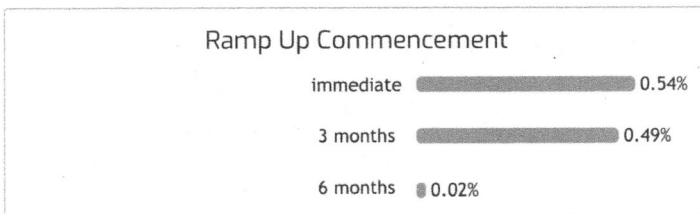

Ramp Up Commencement

immediate   0.54%

3 months   0.49%

6 months   0.02%

Figure 12.1
Current sizing is effective.

initiated using three commencement times, with reference to the buy date: starting immediately, three months later, and six months later. The relatively modest intervals between the three commencement dates indicate that the fund's information advantage is somewhat front-loaded. The results from the three ramp-up commencement times are 0.54% commencing immediately, 0.49% at three months, and 0.02% at six months. All of the ramp-up values are positive, meaning that the more rapid buildup of positions did not improved fund results (i.e., in all three cases, the actual fund results were higher than the counterfactual portfolio). It can also be seen that the positive results decline as the commencement of the ramp-up is delayed. These results suggest that delaying the ramp-up is somewhat advantageous. It seems to benefit a few positions but generally is not better than the current sizing regime. The mild benefit from delaying may be due to a small number of positions underperforming for three to six months and then recovering, a few positions needing more time to hit their full stride, or both.

Takeaways.   Positive results for ramp-up analysis indicate that the fund is building up positions effectively. The investment of more capital sooner actually dampened the fund's returns (i.e., the counterfactual portfolio returns are less than those of the actual fund).

This fund appears to be capturing the vast majority of alpha from its new buys. With this knowledge in hand, the capital allocator is free to redirect attention to investigating other skills. It is worth noting that there may be positions in the fund whose weight is well above the full weight size. The efficacy of these higher weights is not being assessed in this analysis.

The ramp-up results in figure 12.2 indicate that building up new buys to full weight more expeditiously can capture additional excess returns. For this fund, the ramp-up commencement times are immediate, five months

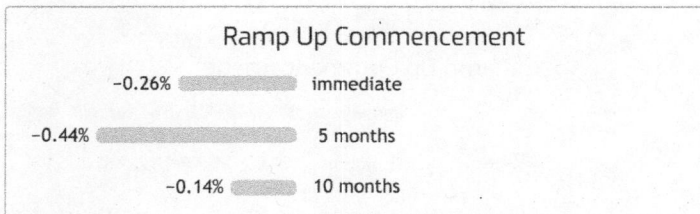

Figure 12.2
Modest opportunity detected.

delayed, and ten months delayed, relative to the initial purchase of new stocks. The results of the three ramp-up commencement times are –0.26% done immediately, –0.44% delaying five months, and –0.14% delaying ten months.

All of the results are modestly negative, indicating that the fund's current sizing regime is fairly effective, although there is an opportunity to put a bit more capital to work across the newer buys. The fund has plenty of time to selectively build up its strongest new buys since the results indicate that the best time to achieve full weight is around five months after initial purchase. These results point to the fund's information advantage being relatively front-loaded. Waiting beyond five months to build up positions appears counterproductive.

Takeaways.   Small negative results from the ramp-up analysis indicate that the fund is generally effective at sizing its new buys. There is a modest alpha enhancement opportunity of 0.44% associated with building up some new buys at or around the five-month mark after their initial purchase. Evaluating the ramp-up results over multiple periods would help in understanding if this skill is consistently good or has changed over time. Moreover, examining it by sector, global region, and financial attribute can indicate if there may be one or two pockets where the lack of ramping up is more costly than suggested by the overall fund results.

This example considers a highly successful fund that has delivered benchmark-beating returns for the trailing ten years. Yet the undersizing of new buys has cost this fund almost 2% annually during the same period. Capturing most or all of this missed alpha could catapult the fund's returns to the top of its peer group. Three different skill investigations are used to explore what's going on and how the fund's consistency or riskiness can be assessed.

The investigation begins with a look at the fund's basic skill results, presented in figure 12.3a. The fund's skills are heavily lopsided. The buy skill is an impressive 6.39%. The sell skill, on the other hand, is essentially neutral at 0.26%. The sizing skill is a different story. It is costing the fund .54% per annum. Fortunately, the impressive buy skill can absorb this alpha drain and still allow the fund to generate a benchmark-beating result of 5.11% (i.e., the fund's relative return is the sum of its skills).

The negative sizing skill may be due to the inadequate initial buildup of positions, poor interim trading (i.e., adds and trims), or a combination of both. A look at the fund's information advantage often helps guide where to look next regarding the cause of the negative sizing skill.

The fund's information advantage is presented in figure 12.3b. This plot contains several strong relative contribution values soon after the average new stock is purchased. New buys tend to generate 2.07 of relative contribution in the forty days immediately after being purchased. An additional 1.28% of relative contribution is captured over the subsequent forty-two days. Relative contribution then goes negative for the remaining three quintiles, with values of –0.51% for the next forty-five days, –0.54% for the subsequent ninety-six days, and –2.30% thereafter. This information advantage is unquestionably powerful and heavily front-loaded. The combination of a strong buy skill together with a front-loaded information advantage suggests that not building up positions sufficiently may play a significant role in the fund's negative overall sizing skill. This is investigated next using ramp-up analysis.

Figure 12.3c shows the results from investigating the more rapid buildup of positions for this fund. The ramp-up results and their corresponding commencement times are –1.67% starting immediately, –1.82% waiting four months, and –1.89% waiting eight months. All of the ramp-up results are negative and substantial. This indicates that close to 2% of incremental alpha can be captured through the faster buildup of new buys (i.e., the counterfactual outperforms the actual fund). Since the potential benefit increases slightly when commencement of the buildup is delayed, this suggests that the fund can take its time to achieve full position weight, up to and including eight months. These results reinforce that ineffective initial sizing is the likely major source of the fund's overall negative sizing skill. Further validation of this conclusion can be obtained by investigating the fund's success with adds and trims (see chapter 10). If the fund's skills in adding and trimming are positive, this would confirm that inadequate initial position sizing is the source of the issue.

Takeaways.   Using some of the newer analytics, it is readily apparent how even highly successful funds may be undermined by a negative skill. Knowing that the fund described is highly dependent on its buy skill and challenged by its sizing skill provides a richer understanding of its return and risk profile. Being dependent on a single skill—even a very strong one—adds a level of uncertainty with regard to repeatability of results. Investigations of all three basic skills, with greater granularity than pursued here, can

(a) Basic Skills

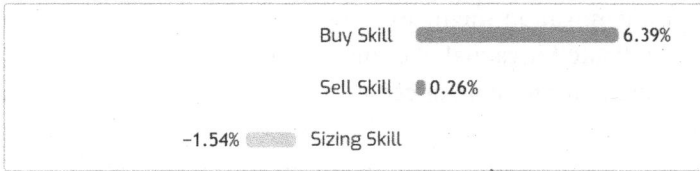

(b) Information Advantage

(c) Ramp Up

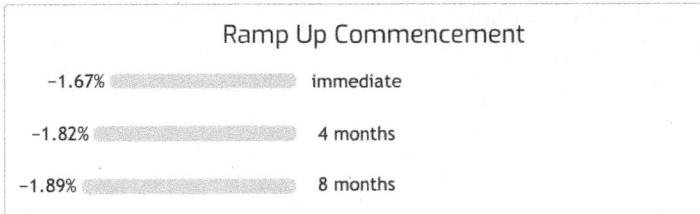

Figures 12.3
Strong buying hides weak sizing opportunity.

help assess the likelihood of the fund continuing to generate excess returns going forward. In particular, it would be helpful to be further assured that the buy skill is consistent over time and across sectors and financial attributes. It would be equally beneficial to confirm that the sizing skill is not highly volatile nor does it appear to be worsening.

This mini case study demonstrates how decision-based skill analysis adds substantially to what can be learned from conventional analytics. Knowing that the past positive results are driven entirely by buying decisions points to the strengths and weaknesses of the fund's alpha generating abilities. Additional investigation might well result in this fund being considered a strong candidate for capital allocation. Alternatively, the skill dynamics surfaced could point to more uncertainty regarding repeatability than may be acceptable.

Conclusion

Fund outperformance is generally built upon strong buying. However, capturing the alpha potential from great buys requires effective position sizing—especially initial position sizing. Basic as this insight seems, precious little is actually known about position sizing and its effective application. The fact is that hundreds of basis points of return are easily lost as the result of undersizing new buys that go on to become strong winners.

Ramp-up analysis offers a means to assess how effectively new buys are being brought up to full weight. This form of analysis can confirm that the existing sizing practices are working well. Alternatively, it can quantify the level of drag that poor sizing decisions are imposing on past results and the risk they pose to future outcomes. Insights like these enable capital allocators to better understand the risk and reward characteristics of a current or potential new fund.

13 Triangulating In on Skill

It is a capital mistake to theorize before one has data.
—Sherlock Holmes

Equity fund assessment is no mean feat. It's far easier to select a fund that goes on to deliver underwhelming results than to choose one that generates alpha. Capital allocators globally nevertheless remain committed to this asset class as a potential source of excess return and diversification. Bringing forth new analytics can enable capital allocators to sharpen their abilities in selecting alpha-generating equity funds.

The previous chapters describe newer analytics that assist capital allocators in better understanding the strengths and shortcomings of equity funds. These analytics deliver crucial insights that are wholly complementary to traditional portfolio analytics. They offer a rich assessment of the manager's judgment and investment processes. They support a more rigorous evaluation of decision repeatability and the likelihood of excess returns going forward. They help in determining who is skilled and who isn't. Their use, it is believed, can help nudge fund assessment closer to a highly skilled and repeatable practice. To the extent this occurs, successful fund allocations may be far less dependent on luck or Holmes-like extraordinary deductions.

This chapter brings together much of what has been discussed thus far into a case study.[1] It begins with a brief description of a successful equity fund that is on the verge of being approved for an allocation. Based on extensive conventional analysis and in-person interviews, the fund meets all the investment requirements and stands out from its closely competitive peers. But before making the final determination, the capital allocator and their search consultant (i.e., the allocation team) want to learn more about what is really driving this fund's results. This additional insight is provided with the help of several newer analytics. The analytics are used to answer the allocation team's questions concerning skills, investment processes, and decision consistency. How each analytic advances the understanding of the fund's buying, sizing, and selling abilities is summarized along the way.

First Among Peers, Perhaps

Upon the conclusion of a recent search, the allocation team for a sophisticated capital allocator has arrived at what they believe to be the best fund from among several finalists. Some of the defining qualities for the chosen fund include:

3.78% relative return annually (past fourteen years)

Thirty-two to thirty-four positions typically held (past five years)

90% approximate turnover annually (past five years)

92% active share on average (past five years)

This fund exhibits many other excellent financial and organizational characteristics. The fund's historic upside capture is 123% and its downside capture is 101%. The results from a host of risk analyses (e.g., tracking error, multifactor alpha, information ratio, Sharpe ratio, Jensen's ratio) were well within comfortable ranges. Attribution analysis confirms the manager's claim that the fund earns most of its excess returns through stock selection. All members of the management team have been with the fund for nine years or more. The fund has assets of $4.5 billion and is not liquidity constrained. Three of the company's other four equity funds consistently outperform their benchmarks, suggesting a strong research and execution culture. The asset management company sponsoring the fund is successful and well capitalized, with solid executive management and an ownership/leadership transition plan in place. The allocation team's due diligence leads them to believe that the fund is an attractive fit for their current allocation needs and that its management is appropriately skilled.

Elevating the Assessment Process

In the past, the level of fund investigation described so far was sufficient for a go- or no-go decision. This time around, the allocation team is choosing to further assess the fund using some of the newer analytics available. A partial description of the additional analytic investigations conducted and the incremental insights this work provided is described below.

Skill Quantification

The fund outperformed its benchmark by 3.78% annually, as mentioned. The allocation team is interested in knowing which skills helped drive this success and which, if any, were a hindrance. The results for the three basic skills for this fund are all positive, as shown in figure 13.1. The buy skill is meaningfully positive at 2.41% annually, over the past fourteen years. The sell skill was less impactful, contributing 0.54% annually to the fund's excess returns. The sizing skill was slightly stronger at 0.83% annually.[2] All three basic skills contributing positively is relatively uncommon.[3] This is a welcome finding that fuels the desire to continue the analysis and learn more.

In particular, the allocation team desires to understand the consistency of the buy skill. They also are interested in assessing if either the sizing or selling skills are in jeopardy of declining or turning negative. There is no single approach to using the newer analytics to find answers to these questions. Instead, it involves investigative probing and follow-up with ever more granular analyses. This use of multiple analytics to uncover as much as possible about each individual skill is referred to as *triangulation*.[4]

Advancement.   The allocation team now is aware that the fund's success is being driven largely by buying with meaningful help from sizing and selling. They turn next to year-by-year analysis to begin understanding the consistency of these skills.

Investigating Consistency

This section examines the consistency of each basic skill. The analyses include fourteen years of fund history.

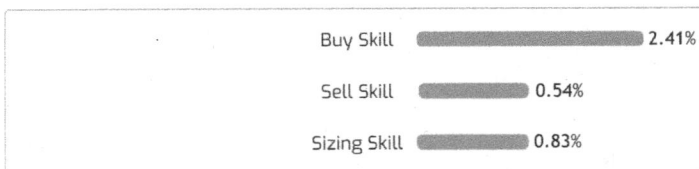

Figure 13.1
Basic skills.

Buy Skill Consistency

The repeatability of the buy skill is examined by looking at this metric on a year-by-year basis. Annual values of the buy skill for the fund are presented in figure 13.2. The buy skill is positive in all but the very first year. The positive values range from a high of 7.95% in 2019 to a low of 0.03% in 2013. The results are somewhat modest during the final three years with an annualized average of 1.10%. The one exception during the history presented is 2011, when the buy skill was −5.28%.

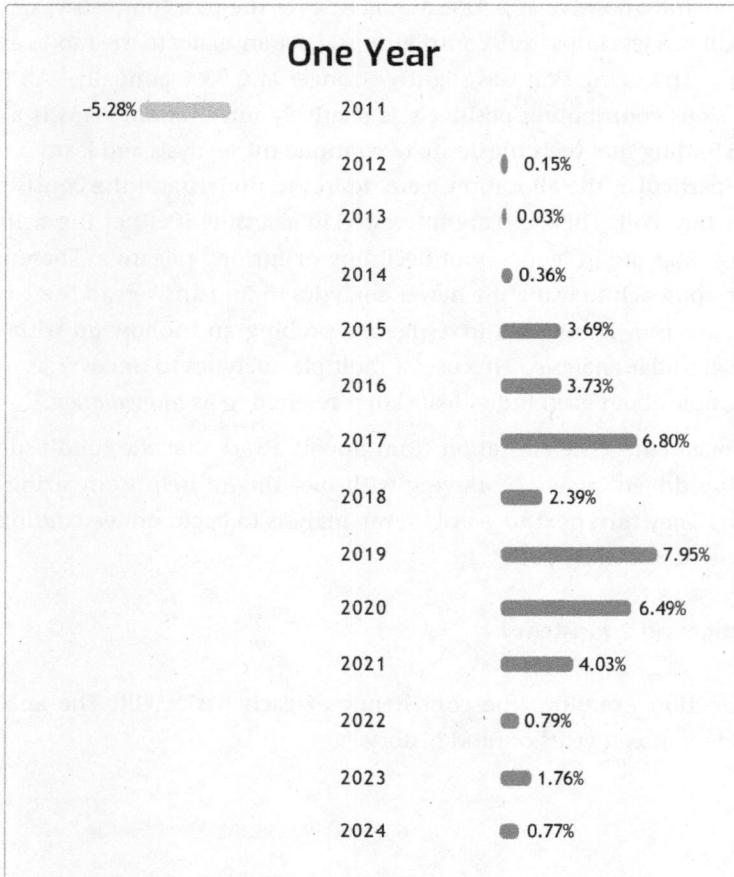

One Year

Year	Value
2011	−5.28%
2012	0.15%
2013	0.03%
2014	0.36%
2015	3.69%
2016	3.73%
2017	6.80%
2018	2.39%
2019	7.95%
2020	6.49%
2021	4.03%
2022	0.79%
2023	1.76%
2024	0.77%

Figure 13.2
Annual buy skills.

Advancement.   The buy skill has been consistently positive over the trailing thirteen years. This bodes well for future success. On the other hand, the magnitude of the buy skill is highly variable. This piques the interest of the allocation team to look at the consistency of the fund's information advantage and buy process. Before that, however, they continue assessing the annual results of the fund's selling and sizing skills.

Sell Skill Consistency

The annual results for the fund's sell skill are presented in figure 13.3. The sell skill is positive eight out of the fourteen years analyzed. The positive

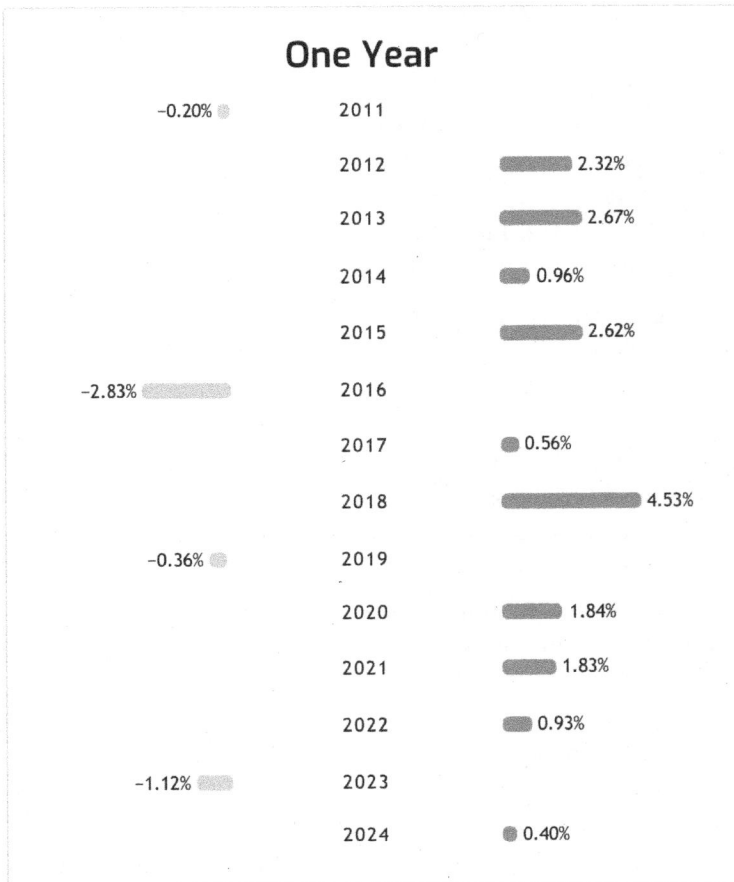

One Year

Year	Value
2011	−0.20%
2012	2.32%
2013	2.67%
2014	0.96%
2015	2.62%
2016	−2.83%
2017	0.56%
2018	4.53%
2019	−0.36%
2020	1.84%
2021	1.83%
2022	0.93%
2023	−1.12%
2024	0.40%

Figure 13.3
Annual sell skills.

values range from 4.53% in 2015 to a low of 0.40% in 2024 (the most recent year). The most negative value was –2.83% computed for 2016. The final three years were mixed with 2023 registering –1.12% and the annualized average across 2022–2024 equaling 0.07%.

Advancement.   The sell skill, the weakest of the three basic skills for this fund, is a bit choppy. The annual sell skill is negative in 29% of the years analyzed. The most recent three-year period is depressed due to the negative value in 2023. The allocation team will be looking at the fund's sell timing and stop-loss analysis to suss out if there is a persistent problem or if selling is simply a bit erratic and should be viewed as a neutral contributor to return versus a source of risk going forward. One upbeat observation is the number of years the sell skill value was in excess of 1%.

Sizing Skill Consistency
Year-by-year results for the sizing skill are presented in figure 13.4. The sizing skill is negative in five of the fourteen years shown. Positive values range from a high of 2.05% in 2022 to a low of 0.11% in 2020. The largest negative value is –2.15% in 2019. The final five years were all positive. The annualized average over the last three years (2022–2024) is 1.43%.

Advancement.   The sizing skill has a bit of a mixed history. Negative values are found in approximately one-third of the years studied. It's worth noting that among the four years with negative results prior to 2017, two were of modest impact: In 2016 the value is virtually zero at –0.09% and in 2012 the negative effect is relatively small at –0.26%. More encouraging is that since 2017 there is only one year with a negative value (2019). All of the most recent five years are positive. The annualized average for the latest three years is 1.43%. The allocation team is cautiously positive regarding the fund's sizing skill and hopes to bolster this assessment a bit by investigating the fund's contribution by size, its skills in initial sizing, and its adds and trims.

Information Advantage

The information advantage or relative contribution by age indicates when, during the life of its ownership, the typical new buy tends to outperform or underperform the fund's average return. The fund's new buys tend to deliver positive relative contribution during months three through fourteen

One Year

	Year	
−0.20%	2011	0.47%
−0.26%	2012	
	2013	0.63%
−0.55%	2014	
−0.63%	2015	
−0.09%	2016	
	2017	0.79%
	2018	0.74%
−2.15%	2019	
	2020	0.11%
−0.69%	2021	
	2022	1.27%
	2023	2.50%
	2024	0.51%

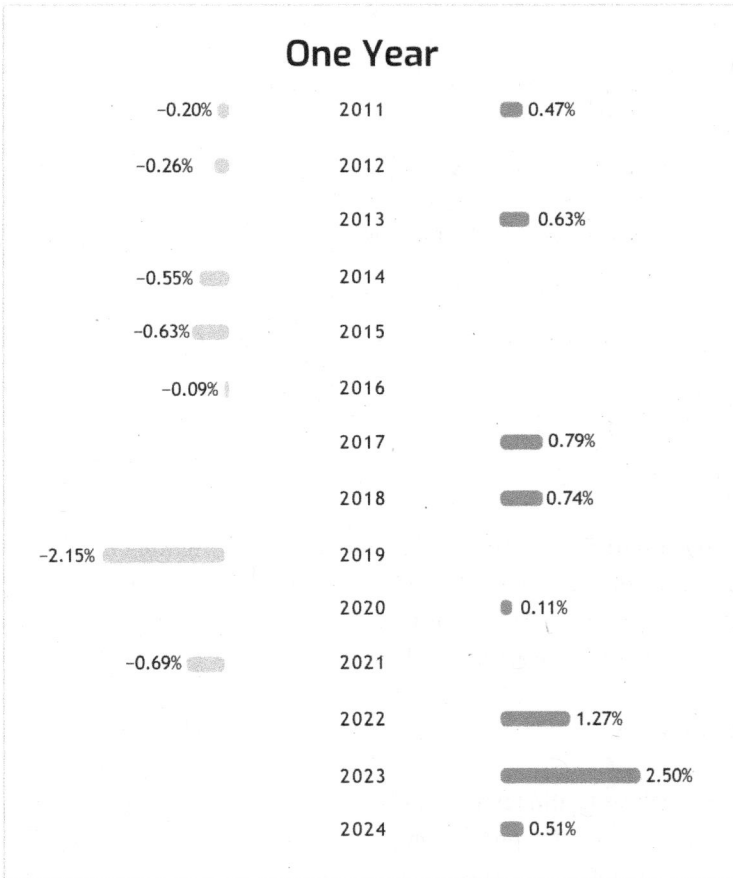

Figure 13.4
Annual sell skills.

subsequent to their initial purchase, as made clear in figure 13.5. The relative contribution is approximately −1.3% for the first and second quintiles (month zero through two months). The relative contribution is positive over the next three quintiles with the strongest results coming in months 8.7 to 14.2.

Advancement.   The fund's new buys reflect a relatively short information advantage, one that appears to peak at around three months after initial purchase and lasts approximately one year. The allocation team now better appreciates the fund's 90% turnover rate, which dovetails with the duration

−1.27%	1 day to 2.5 months
−1.35%	2.5 months to 5.4 months
	5.4 months to 8.7 months 0.62%
	8.7 months to 14.2 months 1.83%
	14.2 months to 113.4 months 0.17%
	Total 0.00%

Figure 13.5
Information advantage.

of the information advantage. After next investigating the buy process, the allocation team will cross-check position sizing by examining contribution by size and reviewing both position ramp up results and how effectively adds and trims are being executed.

Buy Context

Context analysis facilitates assessing the types of stocks being purchased and the consistency of the process employed. Two context analyses reflecting consecutive five-year periods are presented in figure 13.6a covering years 2014–2018 and figure 13.6b representing years 2019–2023. Overall, the buy context or types of stocks the fund is purchasing has remained mostly consistent.

The average one-year volatility for winners is about median for both periods, while losers are now at the fiftieth percentile up modestly from their earlier fortieth percentile. The three-year return levels for winners are again fiftieth percentile in both periods, with the average loser value at the forty-fifth percentile currently, up from the thirtieth percentile earlier. One-year earnings per share growth is about sector median for winners in both periods, while the percentile value for losers is currently seventieth percentile up from fiftieth percentile earlier. The levels for EBITDA to enterprise value have flipped: Winners are now at the eightieth percentile up from the sixtieth

(a)

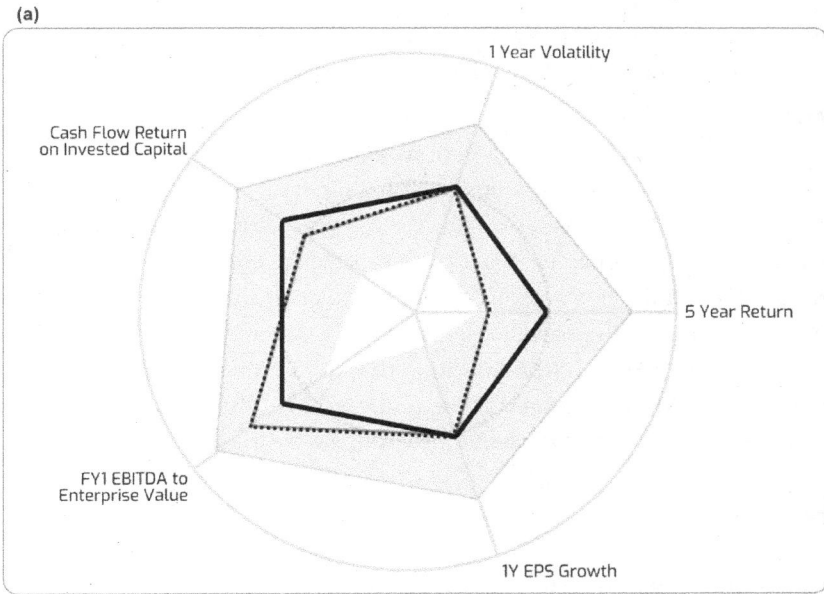

(b)

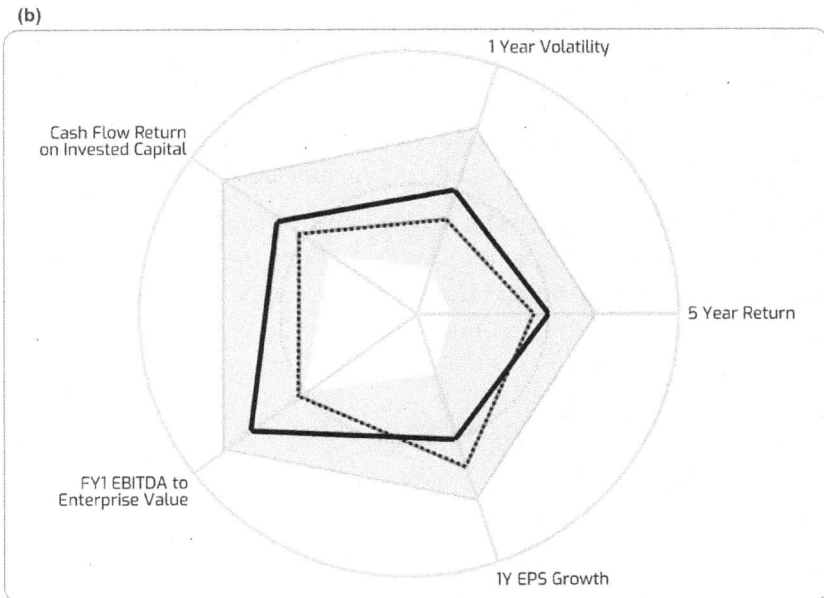

Figure 13.6
a. Earlier buy context. b. Current buy context.

percentile earlier. Losers currently average in the fifty-fifth percentile down from the eightieth percentile five years ago. Finally, the levels of cash-flow return on invested capital are relatively stable for both winners and losers.

Advancement.   The types of stocks being targeted are fairly consistent over the two consecutive five-year periods examined. This consistency bodes well for continued successful buying going forward. The most notable shifts over time are higher levels of trailing three-year returns among losing purchases currently, higher levels of earnings per share among losing buys more recently, and a flip in the levels of EBITDA to enterprise value with winners now in the eightieth percentile while earlier losers were at this level. There does not appear to be a clear indication that any of these changes have negatively impacted the buy skill. These results will be discussed with the fund management team to understand if the shifts were intentional.

Ramp Up

Ramp-up analysis is used to evaluate if new buys are being built up sufficiently and in a timely manner.[5] The ramp-up analysis results for the fund, presented in figure 13.7, indicate that overall new buys are being built up effectively. However, there is a modest opportunity to capture 0.53% of additional excess return if more undersized positions are taken to full size soon after their initial purchase (i.e., commencing immediately). This finding is consistent with the relatively short duration of the fund's information advantage.

Advancement.   Overall, new buys generally are being built up effectively. In particular, initial sizing appears to be capturing the early price opportunities identified by the fund's information advantage. The allocation team concludes that initial sizing is more than satisfactory.

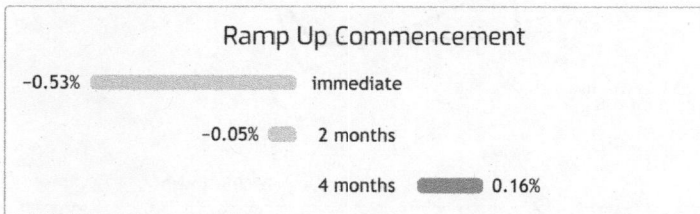

Figure 13.7
Initial sizing skill.

Contribution by Size

This analysis highlights the relative return from positions based on their absolute (total) size. The most eye-catching detail in figure 13.8 is that the largest positions (fifth quintile) generate the greatest relative contribution at 1.66%, which means that the manager's highest conviction bets are paying off nicely.

Advancement. The contribution by size results show that the highest conviction positions are outperforming the fund's average returns. These results give further confidence concerning the fund's sizing skills. In particular, they show that the manager tends to identify strong positions and size these holdings meaningfully.

Adds and Trims

The examination of adds and trims quantifies the impact of interim trading (trades between initial buy and selling). The results of the fund's add and trim analysis are shown in figure 13.9. Three of the skills have positive values, indicating that they are helping fund results. The exception is adding to winners, which has a value of –0.44%. This negative result shows that at least some adds to winners are poorly timed—most likely being made as these positions begin to lose their alpha generating abilities. A common reason for such ineffective capital allocations concerns the management

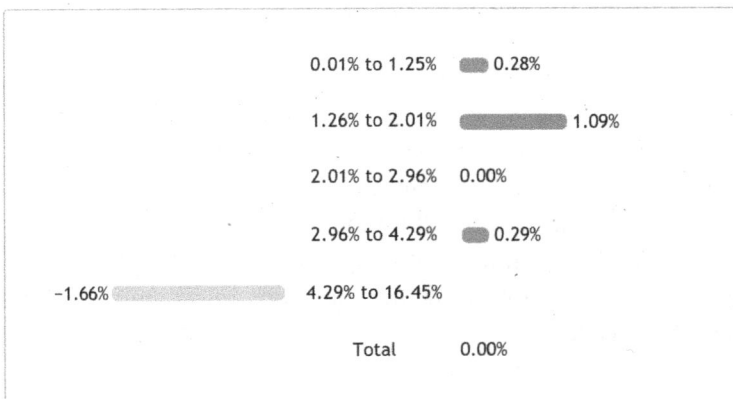

0.01% to 1.25%	0.28%
1.26% to 2.01%	1.09%
2.01% to 2.96%	0.00%
2.96% to 4.29%	0.29%
4.29% to 16.45%	–1.66%
Total	0.00%

Figure 13.8
Contribution by size.

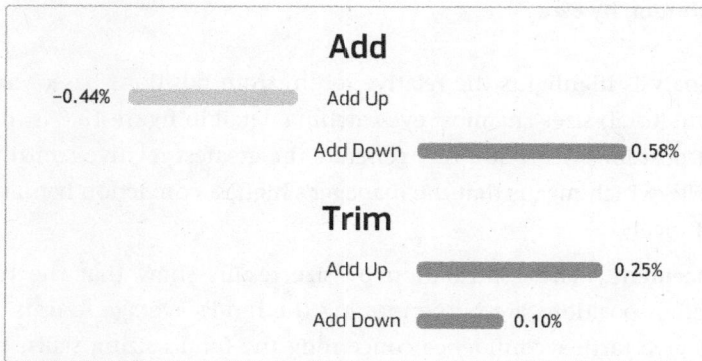

Figure 13.9
Adds and trims.

of inflows. Frequently, inflows are parked temporarily in the fund's most liquid stocks upon receipt, with the intention that this capital will be redeployed more strategically over the subsequent few days or weeks. Far too often, the initial step is taken and the second step gets lost in the hubbub of day-to-day fund management. This type of partially executed plan can lead to the misallocation of capital that undermines fund results.

Advancement. The fund's skill in position sizing is further confirmed by the add and trim results. The fund generally captures incremental alpha as it trades around position size. The allocation team concludes that the add and trim skills are effective while noting that they will monitor any further decline in the results from adding to winners.

Sell Timing

Sell timing analysis is used to evaluate if young positions are being sold prematurely and if older positions are being held beyond their ability to generate excess returns.[6] The sell timing results for the fund are presented in figure 13.10. The timing of sells appears to be working in that three of the results are positive (meaning these decisions are helpful). The selling of younger losers is slightly negative at −0.02% (effectively zero). These results are consistent with the basic sell skill reviewed above.

Advancement. It was observed earlier that the overall sell skill is modest and the year-by-year sell skill is a bit erratic. The sell timing analysis does

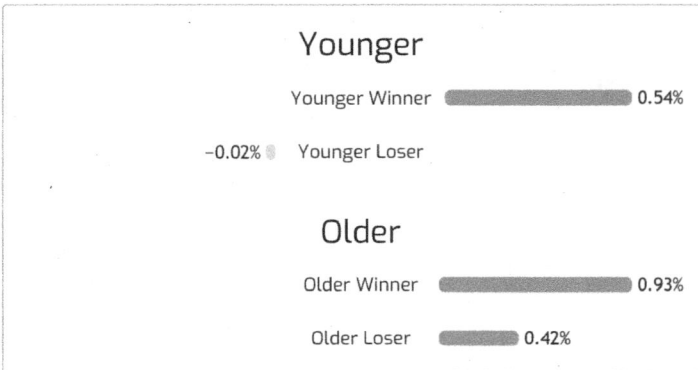

Figure 13.10
Sell timing.

not point to any persistent ineffective sell tendencies, which, if present, would be indicated by meaningfully negative values in one or more of the four sell timing skills analyzed. The allocation team surmises that while selling is not the fund's strong suit, there does not appear to be a looming risk of this skill deteriorating any time soon.

Management of Substantial Losers

The analysis of substantial losers sheds light on whether positions that have experienced a meaningful price decline are being harvested effectively or if they are being allowed to further drag down fund results. This type of analysis is referred to colloquially as *stop-loss analysis*. Results from analyzing the fund's management of substantial losers are presented in figure 13.11. These positions appear to be managed very effectively. All results are positive. There is no detectable benefit to the fund from advancing the sale of these positions for any of the three thresholds examined (i.e., down 20%, 30%, or 40%).

Advancement.   Similar to the results from the sell timing analysis, this analysis of substantial losers does not point to any persistent issues with the fund's selling—or in this case not selling these positions. The allocation team has concluded that, over time, selling is more likely to generate slightly positive or neutral results versus having a significant negative impact on the fund.

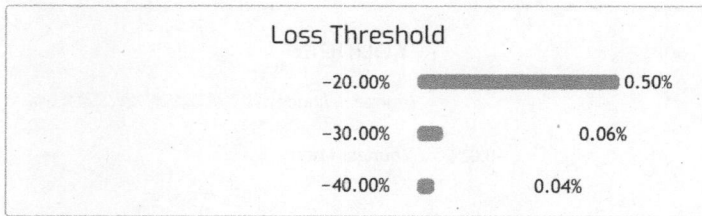

Figure 13.11
Management of significant losers.

Final Vote

The fund being considered ranked strongly based on conventional analytics. It has delivered attractive total and relative returns, compared very favorably with its closest peers, and done so with acceptable levels of risk. This fund meets or exceeds the criteria used in previous fund selections.

Deeper investigations using the newer analytics further support the allocation team's initial appraisal. It's now understood that the fund's attractive results are being driven by its buy skill, which has been positive for the past thirteen years. The types of stocks the fund is purchasing reflect a consistent set of financial attributes (or factor signature), indicating a consistent approach to sourcing new names. Although less impactful, the fund's sizing and selling also contribute positively to total returns. The fund appears to possess a relatively short information advantage of roughly one year. The manager's initial sizing decisions and turnover are in sync with this dynamic. The timing of sells suggests that the manager is skilled in knowing when positions are tired versus when they possess additional alpha generating ability. Interim trading (adds and trims) and substantial losers are being managed successfully. The fund's largest capital bets are generating the highest returns, as indicated by the contribution by size analysis. All investigation results point to skilled decision-making generally and the existence of effective investment processes—all of which support continued alpha going forward.

The allocation team votes unanimously to approve this fund and provide it with a significant capital allocation. Their investment summary to the board of directors and other oversight groups is much stronger than those in the past. Their recommendation is full of specific skill and investment process measures, and their convictions are backed by a deep understanding of which decisions are driving this fund's results. The allocation team is maintaining a list of key metrics to monitor, based largely on the newer analytics, which will provide forewarnings of process changes and/or skill deterioration. The allocation team intends to use these early indicators to intervene where appropriate. This may take the form of inquiries such as: Why do skills and processes appear to be changing? Are the changes intentional? Deteriorations in skill and process might even signal that this fund needs to be completely reassessed. And such a reassessment can be initiated well before skill and process declines impact fund returns.

In summary, the allocation team sees that their assessment process is now stronger and more efficient. They know not only how this fund performed but which skills and processes are responsible for the performance. The improved underwriting provided by integrating the newer analytics into the fund assessment process leads the allocation team to consider both reassessing the other current allocations and possibly expanding the number of funds in their equity program.

14 Skill Analytics

Investment skill is the raison d'être of the asset management industry; managers sell it and clients pay for it. In spite of this, empirical evidence of its existence, and what it looks like in practice, is sparse; in fact, there is a mountain of words, papers and opinions arguing that it's as likely to be spotted as the extinct dodo.
—Rick Di Mascio

Fund assessment is supported by a plethora of services. Only a few, however, use decision-based analytics to identify and quantify skill. Summaries of decision-based offerings are presented, followed by a sampling of other services that support fund selection.

Decision-Based Analytics
The following firms offer products that use decision-based analytics. They are listed in order of their date of establishment.

Inalytics Ltd.
Founded in 1998, Inalytics has, from its beginning, supported capital allocators with fund selection and monitoring and helped fund managers improve their investment decisions. In 2022, Inalytics introduced a significant enhancement to their analytics with DECSIS, which they define as a skill-based attribution methodology. According to Inalytics, DECSIS is wholly aligned to the way high conviction equity managers make decisions by focusing on what the company sees as the two critical steps in the investment process: decisions on what to own and how much of it to own while the stock is in the portfolio.

DECSIS begins by analyzing some seven hundred different types of investment decisions using summary-level attribution. Deeper investigations then provide insights into decision-based skills, including individual research or buys, sizing, and trades decisions for each position held in a fund. The DECSIS analytics and services reflect the company's firsthand experience in applying concepts from behavioral finance to more than a thousand institutional portfolios.[1] This work has led Inalytics to determine that funds that outperform do so primarily due to the two skills mentioned above.

Complimenting the depth of its data analytics background, Inalytics believes that improvement comes through working with clients to help them understand their individual strengths and weaknesses.

Further information regarding Inalytics and their fund analytics is available at www.inalytics.com.

FactSet Research Systems Inc.

In 2004 Cabot Investment Technology Inc. was founded to develop and market analytics for the active equities industry. In June 2021 Cabot became a wholly owned subsidiary of FactSet Research Systems Inc. FactSet now offers the Cabot equity fund analytics on their global multiasset platform.[2] The Cabot analytics use decision-based inputs to quantify manager skills, investment processes, and behavioral tendencies. These analytics are used by capital allocators for fund selection and by fund managers to become more self-aware and improve.

The Cabot analytics are based on a decision representation referred to as an *action*. Actions reflect the strategic decisions made to alter a fund's composition; decisions are then implemented through trades.[3] An analytic known as a *counterfactual portfolio* is employed to assess which actions consistently add to fund excess returns (positive skills) and which detract from fund excess returns (negative skills).[4] Additional analytics such as machine learning, linear algebra, and optimization routines are used to compute other metrics.

The Cabot analytics provide considerable granularity that helps in assessing skill magnitude and consistency. Skills can be investigated over varying periods (e.g., inception to date, annually, rolling multiyear), by sector or global region (e.g., consumer durables, financials), and by relatively high and low stock/company exposures to financial factors (e.g., earnings growth, debt-to-asset, price momentum). The software supports investigations into skills using multiple analytic perspectives. For example, the selling skill can be interrogated by considering the basic sell skill, skill based on sell timing, and skill at managing substantial losers (i.e., stop-loss analysis). This ability to triangulate skills from multiple perspectives provides deep confidence in truly ascertaining what's working and what's not.[5] FactSet-Cabot has analyzed over six hundred funds and published numerous academic and professional journal articles based on their research results.

Further information on the FactSet-Cabot software is available at www .factset.com.

Alpha Theory LLC

Since 2006, portfolio management and optimization software company Alpha Theory has helped investment managers codify their position sizing processes to capture more of their research alpha and deliver insights that can be used to measure and improve manager skill.

Their software product, Alpha Engine, provides a framework for managers to optimize their best ideas in real time by integrating customized investment rules with the outputs of their research process, including price targets, conviction levels, and other analyst inputs. Alpha Engine has been applied to over 500 funds involving more than 1,000 research analysts and 1 million price targets.

The company's ten-plus years of research show that funds often pick the right stocks but size them ineffectively, which leads to −400 basis points of annual slippage that could be easily captured through more disciplined position sizing.

At the time of writing, Alpha Theory is not directly supporting equity fund selection. However, the company is receiving requests from capital allocators for their process discipline scores and skill metrics to provide unique insights that investors are not able to access elsewhere.

Further information about Alpha Theory can be found at www.alphatheory .com.

Essentia Analytics Ltd.

Founded in 2013, Essentia provides analytic support to equity fund managers and capital allocators. The company offers a product known as Insight that helps capital allocators better understand the skills of fund managers and assists fund managers in improving. The Insight product assesses seven distinct manager decisions: stock picking, entry timing, sizing, scaling in, size adjusting, scaling out, and exit timing.

The Essentia marketing materials indicate they use the profitability of a position in quantifying skill. They term this value the *position-level alpha*. It is computed as the profit/(loss) generated by a position over its holding period relative to a similar amount of capital having been invested in the fund's benchmark (i.e., a passive or average return). Position level data, trading data, corporate actions, and daily pricing data are used in computing these position-level alphas.

Essentia's skill metrics include both a batting average and slugging ratio based on the position-level alphas. The batting average is computed as the number of positions with positive alphas divided by the total number of positions. The slugging ratio is computed as the average gain from positions with a positive alpha divided by the average loss from positions with a negative alpha. These two metrics are used to help determine a manager's skill level or a fund's desirability. Essentia also supports the compilation or overlay of multiple position histories (which they refer to as episodes) to visualize aggregate affects and trends. It is unclear how skill values are computed for the individual manager decisions defined by Essentia.

Further information regarding Essentia and their skill analytics are available at www.essentia-analytics.com.

Behaviour Lab Ltd.

Founded in 2016, Behaviour Lab develops products that enhance decision-making for investment professionals across equity, fixed income, and multi-asset products. Deeply steeped in behavioral science, the company provides both rich analytics and a robust process for helping implement improved decision making. The company's primary products are Polygon and Vertex, which support both capital allocators and fund managers.

Polygon is an analytic engine that performs extensive analyses of decisions and decision patterns. Among its unique abilities is the combined assessment of when a decision is made, why it was made, and how effectively the decision achieved its intended result. The Polygon results are based on over one hundred analytical modules that dissect complex decisions into smaller components, such as timing, context, and economic environment. Vertex integrates client behavioral data with analytic results from Polygon to enable capital allocators to make more effective allocation decisions, helping them make choices that are better aligned with their intentions. This includes over eighty decision-alignment and debiasing tools. Behaviour Lab software is used by a variety of capital allocators to assess their allocation decisions as well as investigate the skills of internal and external equity funds.

Behaviour Lab has supported over three hundred equity funds with their intensive learn and improve services. Their analyses indicate that funds typically can improve by over 250 basis points through their collaborations. The company has published articles in academic and professional journals regarding their analytics and strategies for behavioral improvement.

For further information, visit www.behaviourlab.com.

Observation

The companies listed above and their analytics are making great inroads toward establishing real skill metrics across active management. More innovation is likely as more firms are providing new and alternative approaches to decision-based skill measurement. Capital allocators can accelerate the development of a broader and even more helpful set of skill analytics simply by requiring that asset managers provide some of the newer analytics as part of the due diligence process and as a part of ongoing client services. Academics and consultants can foster the adoption of the newer analytics through studying and reporting on the relative merits of the various offerings. To the extent that fund managers embrace the newer analytics to help calibrate and improve their skills, all will go even faster.

Other Fund Assessment Services

A wide range of analytic and data services support the fund assessment process. Some provide explicit fund ratings, others data and analytics for investigating funds, and some provide both. The listing below is not intended to be complete but only to indicate the range of products and services now available that are built upon conventional (or nondecision-based) analytics.

Morningstar Research Services LLC

The name Morningstar is synonymous with fund ratings. They've been providing the well-known star ratings for mutual funds since 1985. Their best-known product is Morningstar Direct, which includes the star ratings, extensive conventional analytics, and a vast amount of fund descriptive information. Some of the details available for each fund include returns, risk, funds style, peer group comparisons, share classes, fund sponsors, and holdings information. The star ratings are based on historical data. Morningstar Direct is used to help in fund screening and surveillance.

Morningstar launched its fund research analyst ratings in 2011. The analyst ratings provide a forward-looking, qualitative, and predictive assessment of fund attractiveness. These ratings express an analyst's conviction in a fund's go-forward investment merits based on a combination of fundamental research and conventional portfolio analytics. Only a fraction of funds receive analyst ratings. In order to provide more forward-looking fund assessments, Morningstar introduced its quantitative ratings system in 2017. The quantitative ratings use machine learning to replicate the decision processes of the research analysts and provide full coverage of all equity (and other) funds. The forward-looking ratings receive ranks of Gold, Silver, Bronze, Neutral, and Negative. These ratings are also available through Morningstar Direct. In total, Morningstar provides ratings for 3,300 unique equity strategies globally. (A strategy may be used to support multiple funds or products, such as mutual fund, active ETF, and SMA).

Morningstar also makes available its extensive fund database, which is used by a great many capital allocators. This data can be efficiently queried using Python notebooks, which are provided by Morningstar and are programmed to answer a wide variety of common inquiries from capital allocators and consultants. Their extensive database and ready access make Morningstar a popular reference source for many capital allocators, consultants, financial advisors, and individual investors.

For more information about the Morningstar products and services, go to www.morningstar.com.

CFRA Holdings LLC

CFRA was founded in 1994 and has been in the fund ratings business since 2009, when it acquired the mutual fund and ETF research business line of Standard & Poor's. CFRA develops its fund ratings by combining conventional fund analytics with in-depth holdings analyses, performed by credit/equity research analysts. The holdings analyses include estimates of the credit worthiness of the underlying company, projected cash flows, and an assessment of the current stock price to its intrinsic value. Low fees and low fund turnover are viewed favorably in the ratings method.

For more information about CFRA and its ratings, go to www.cfraresearch .com.

Touring Technology Associates LLC

Touring was founded in 2016 to apply artificial intelligence to fund analysis and investment. They use their technology to identify the best names held in equity funds and then build "best buys" portfolios. Touring's Hercules software replicates what mutual funds are likely to hold currently and in the future, based on their prior public filings. A second analytic, called Ensemble Alpha, then chooses the holdings across a group of funds that are the most likely to outperform going forward.

The Touring materials suggest that its technology can identify which funds are doing well based on skill versus luck. This ability is currently in beta testing with financial advisors, and not available commercially as of this writing.[6]

Further information about Touring is available at www.turingtechnology associates.com.

Lipper/London Stock Exchange Group (LSEG)

Lipper has been providing fund ratings and other financial information since the early1970s. Lipper uses a combination of conventional analytics (e.g., information ratio, relative return, style, tracking error) to formulate individual fund ranks relative to their Lipper Peer Group constituents. Top-ranked funds are given the designation of Lipper Leaders.

More about Lipper can be found at www.lseg.com.

15   Conclusion

The secret of getting ahead is getting started.
—Mark Twain

It's About Time

The active management industry is in need of a significant rethinking about skill. There are no generally accepted definitions in use today regarding what skill looks like or how it should be computed. The absence of clarity on these fundamental concepts is one reason for the often-heard query: Was it skill or luck? This question itself underscores how poorly skill is understood. Skill and luck are not mutually exclusive. Rather, they are end points on a single continuum. So the more appropriate question capital allocators should be asking is: Where on this skill–luck continuum does a particular manager or fund fall?

The current skill knowledge deficit needs to be reversed, and the sooner, the better. Doing this will require a good bit of industry conversation, debate, innovation, and compromise. It will also involve unlearning things we know that aren't so, especially concerning the appropriate uses for conventional analytics and the availability of skilled managers. It's a big job and will take some time to accomplish. It's about time we get started.

Final Thoughts

Interest in actively managed equities is enormous. Capital allocators have invested (and continue to invest) tens of trillions of dollars in this asset class in hopes of capturing excess returns and achieving greater portfolio diversification. A number of capital allocators are successfully capturing excess returns through their active equity allocations and doing so regularly. Their success is due in part to adopting new ways of thinking about what they want from these allocations. Among these refinements are giving individual managers more leeway in their fund construction, requiring less benchmark tracking, and deemphasizing short-term fund results in favor of long-term success across their entire active equities programs.

Capital allocators are now able to be more exacting in their fund assessments by incorporating some of the newer analytics into the fund assessment process. These newer analytics use decision-based inputs to identify and quantify skills. They capture the cause and effect between decisions and returns that is crucial to meaningful skill measurements. They are benefiting from more fact-based skill information and are less reliant upon hunches or intuitions. They know more about each fund investigated and are making better allocation decisions.

There are many actively managed equity funds that regularly outperform their benchmarks. This is among the findings from five of the industry's top decision-based analytics providers. Their research points to a large group of elite funds that generate meaningful excess returns more often than not. Moreover, it is highly likely that many more such elite funds exist outside of the several thousand that these companies have so far analyzed. Key among their findings is that the manager's skill in buying stocks is what primarily drives excess returns. Therefore, it is in the best interest of capital allocators to fully understand a fund's buying prowess. This includes the use of rigorously formulated metrics that quantify the buy skill and provide measures of its consistency.

The newer analytics have been brought to market using a variety of mathematical approaches. Each approach uses decisions to identify skills, quantify their impact on fund results, and assess their repeatability. The range of skills being measured include the three basic skills (buy, sell, sizing), a fund's information advantage, effectiveness of sell timing, impacts from interim trading (adds, trims), management of substantial losers, and initial position sizing adequacy. The newer analytics are also delivering insights into a fund's profitability of position episodes, investment processes, skills by sector, skills by financial attribute, and skills over time. The analysis of decision context and behavioral tendencies also helps inform capital allocation decisions.

Combining results from the newer analytics with those provided by conventional analytics enables the most rigorous assessments of a fund's skills. Moreover, investigating each skill with several of the newer analytics allows capital allocators to triangulate the strength and durability of buying, selling, and sizing abilities. This leads to a better understanding as to whether any individual decision type is a likely future alpha contributor or a potential source of risk.

Active management skills have been poorly understood for over a hundred years. Prevailing conventional analytics deliver valuable verification of how a fund generated its past performance. These analytics sometimes hint at the presence of skill but fall well short of actually quantifying skills. Shifting toward the integration of the newer decision-based analytics can allow capital allocators to make more informed allocation decisions. This can lead to stronger results across their active equity programs. This shift offers the potential for fund managers themselves to learn and improve— thereby increasing the number of elite funds available to capital allocators. Moreover, a more robust and more transparent active management industry will undoubtedly alter the ultimate equilibrium point between actively managed and passively managed equities. Transitioning to greater use of the newer analytics offers substantial potential benefits for capital allocators, asset managers, and investors generally. It's about time the industry begins discussing what's missing in today's skill knowledge and what can be done to improve this situation.

Acknowledgments

My sincere thanks to my friend Andrew Tuttle, whose deep knowledge of equity management helped tremendously in the development of this book. Andrew has a truly uncommon ability to see what others miss within analytic results and to then relay this information in a clear and very understandable fashion. A special thanks go out to Sangeeta Reddy for her friendship and unwavering help in completing this endeavor. It is with deep gratitude that I acknowledge the unflagging support of Robert Robie throughout my tenure at FactSet. Thanks also to Nicholas Clainos, whose enthusiasm and friendship have been of invaluable help as I prepared for and undertook this writing. Thanks to Kyra Spradlin and Jeanne LaFrance for their brilliant art direction and editing. Thanks also to Michael Acton for his helpful commentary on earlier versions of this book.

The love and support of family and friends has been invaluable during this process. Their enthusiasm and encouragement spurred me on, especially in those rare moments when what loomed ahead seemed unending. A special thanks to my daughter Joy for her unwavering support and love—you are the best.

My heartfelt thanks to the following individuals, who generously provided tremendous insights that influenced my thinking and shaped the content of this book. Their contributions are greatly appreciated, as is the energy and inquisitiveness they brought to each conversation: Jack Behar, Jeannine Caruso, Siew Kai Choy, Dan DiBartolomeo, Rick Di Mascio, Stephen Dover, Matthew Gadsden, Carrie Green, Emily Haisley, Liz Hecht, Cameron Hight, Arjun Kumar, Janet Larsen, Stephen Lister, Brooks Macdonald, Michael Mauboussin, Eoin Murry, Terrance Odean, Maarten Slendebroek, Magdalena Smith, Timothy Strauts, Jonas Svallin, Corrado Tiralongo, Whyly Tollette, Willard Umphrey, and Jay Willoughby.

Notes

Chapter 1

1. The term *capital allocators*, as used throughout this book, refers to the diverse group of institutional and professional asset owners and allocators. Included in this group are sovereign wealth funds, pension funds, foundations, endowments, family offices, outsourced chief investment officers (OCIO), insurance companies, and banks.

2. Michael A. Ervolini, *Managing Equity Portfolios: A Behavioral Approach to Improving Skills and Investment Processes* (MIT Press, 2014).

3. SPIVA Global Scorecard, "SPIVA Mid-Year report 2024," S&P Global, S&P Dow Jones, Fall 2024.

4. The term *alpha* as used here refers to its colloquial meaning of excess return or the difference between a fund's return and that of its benchmark. The more technically correct definition of alpha is a measure of risk-adjusted return, based on a regression analysis involving a fund's return series and one or more risk factors.

Chapter 2

1. William F. Sharpe, "The Arithmetic of Active Management," *Financial Analyst Journal* 47 (1991): 7–9.

2. Eugene F. Fama, "Efficient Capital Markets: A Review of Theory and Empirical Work," *Journal of Finance* 25 (1969): 383–417.

3. This individual ran a very large active global equity group that regularly delivered excess returns, over decades.

4. Nicholas Megaw and Will Schmitt, "Tech Boom Forces US Funds to Dump Shares to Avoid Breach of Tax Rules," *Financial Times*, October 25, 2024.

5. "Investment Skill: Does It Exist and What Does It Look Like?," Inalytics Ltd., Spring 2022, Research Paper no. 14, https://inalytics.com; Klakow Akepanidtaworn,

Rick Di Mascio, Alex Imas, and Lawrence D. W. Schmidt, "Selling Fast and Buying Slow: Heuristics and Trading Performance of Institutional Investors," *Journal of Finance* 78 (December 2023): 3055–3098, https://doi.org/10.1111/jofi.13271.

6. Alpha Theory LLC primarily assists long-short equity hedge funds in improving their position sizing skills and processes. Behaviour Lab Ltd. provides equity, fixed income, and multiasset investors with fund analytics and tools to help change behaviors and make better decisions. Essentia Analytics Ltd. offers broader skill assessments similar to those of Inalytics Ltd. and FactSet-Cabot, a subsidiary of FactSet Research Inc. More about the offerings of these firms is presented in chapter 14. Billy Armfield and Cameron Hight, "The 10-Year Streak: Alpha Theory 2021 Year in Review," February 25, 2022; Chris Woodcock, Alesi Rowland. and Snežana Pejić, "The Alpha Life Cycle: New Insight into Investment Alpha and How Portfolio Managers Can Sustain It," *Journal of Investing* 31 (October 2022): 27–35.

7. William F. Sharpe, "Determining a Fund's Effective Asset Mix," *Investment Management Review* 2 (September/October 1988): 59–69.

8. John Rekenthaler, Michele Gambera, and Joshua Charlson, "Estimating Portfolio Style: A Comparative Study of Portfolio-Based Fundamental Analysis and Returns-Based Style Analysis," Morningstar Research, January 2004.

9. This objective being subject to normal constraints such as overconcentration and liquidity.

Chapter 3

1. As an added bonus, these newer analytics also enable fund managers to become more self-aware, improve, and earn fees commensurate with their differentiated value.

2. William F. Sharpe, "The Sharpe Ratio," *Journal of Portfolio Management* 21 (Fall 1994): 49–58; Martijn Cremers and Antti Petajisto, "How Active Is Your Fund Manager? A New Measure That Predicts Performance," International Center for Finance at the Yale School of Management, March 2009; Eugene F. Fama and Kenneth R. French, "Luck Versus Skill in the Cross-Section of Mutual Fund Returns," *Journal of Finance* 65 (October 2010): 1915–1947.

3. Michael A. Ervolini, "Motivated Reasoning," in *Managing Equity Portfolios* (MIT Press, 2014).

4. Attribution analysis can also extend to the assessment of a fund's exposure to risk factors as well. Risk attribution quantifies how much of a fund's excess returns are the result of specific risk exposures, such as growth, value, interest rates, energy, and so on. The discussion presented here focuses exclusively on basic attribution.

5. Sharpe, "The Sharpe Ratio."

6. Cremers and Petajisto, "How Active Is Your Fund Manager?"

7. Martijn Cremers, "Active Share and the Three Pillars of Active Management: Skill, Conviction and Opportunity," *Financial Analyst Journal* 73 (2016): 61–79.

8. Fama and French, "Luck Versus Skill."

9. Jonathan B. Berk and Richard C. Greene, "Mutual Fund Flows and Performance in Rational Markets," *Journal of Political Economy* 112 (2004): 1269–1295. See also Jonathon B. Berk, "Five Myths of Active Portfolio Management," *Journal of Portfolio Management* 31 (Spring 2005): 27–31.

10. Randolph B. Cohen, Joshua D. Coval, and Lubos Pastor, "Judging Fund Managers by the Company They Keep," *Journal of Finance* 60 (2005): 1057–1096.

Chapter 4

1. In finance, linked returns commonly refer to the geometric linking of returns over subperiods to calculate time-weighted rates of return. In the current discussion the subperiods are daily. Linking the daily returns is computed as: $(1+r)_1 (1+i)_2 \ldots (1+i)_j$, where $(_j)$ denotes the final day in the time series.

2. This last question concerns the familiar trope that active managers should be long-term investors and therefore their funds should reflect long holding periods and low rates of turnover by name. The obvious shortcoming of this belief is that it assumes that all funds have the same or nearly the same information advantage. Or perhaps more correctly, such a belief is simply inconsistent with the idea of an information advantage in the first place. For surely if the concept of an information advantage resonates, and can be quantified, then the length of each manager's information advantage should inform how long positions are held and the level of name turnover that might be expected.

Chapter 5

1. I am deeply grateful to FactSet Research Systems Inc. for providing extensive access to and use of their software application for identifying and quantifying equity manager skill. This application is known as Cabot Behavioral Analytics as of the time of this writing.

2. The analyses considered in this book focus exclusively on long equities, ignoring other positions held by funds. Regarding analytic complexity, consider that a single position may experience both an add and a trim on the same day. It can occur if early in the day a new position is purchased and this purchase is funded by trimming existing positions; and then later that day the fund receives an inflow that is allocated across some or all of then-current positions. One or more positions might be trimmed in the morning and then be added to in the afternoon.

3. This visualization denotes actions as a single event; in actuality, the event illustrated may be the result of multiple related actions. For example, a new buy initiated on March 1 may involve four or five incremental purchases before achieving the desired allocation or fund weight. This short series of buys would be combined and presented as a single buy whose weight equals the sum of all the incremental purchases. By analyzing the actual fund's history, it is possible to suss out the average number of days it takes a fund to complete a new buy, an add, a trim, or a final sell. Presenting associated actions as a single action facilitates a better understanding of what strategic decisions the manager made and their impact on fund results.

Chapter 6

1. Other methods for sussing out skill are discussed in chapter 15.

2. The passive weight (benchmark weight plus equal share of total active weight) is sometimes modulated so that slightly more active weight is given to larger benchmark positions and slightly less active weight given to smaller benchmark positions. This additional adjustment may make the establishment of each buy's passive weight more consistent with the fund's actual sizing practices.

3. How swiftly or slowly a fund realizes the desired initial position weight depends upon the size of the position being established, the stock's daily trading volume, and the fund's demonstrated tolerance for market impact (i.e., percent of daily trading volume).

4. The weights of positions in the counterfactual portfolio may also be modulated due to subsequent buys being initialized with passive weights that differ from their fund weights. When passive weights are larger than fund weights, the difference is funded by trimming all other positions in the counterfactual portfolio on that day. Likewise, when the passive weight is less than the fund weight, the difference is reallocated to all other positions then in the counterfactual portfolio. For example, if a position's fund weight were 3% and the passive weight for the counterfactual portfolio were 5%, the new buy in the counterfactual portfolio requires additional capital. This additional capital is obtained by trimming all other positions in the counterfactual portfolio by 2% on a pro rata basis.

5. Passive selling can be accomplished with the use of a fixed holding period. This approach would result in each active buy being sold once it was in the counterfactual portfolio for the fixed holding period. One method for establishing the length of the fixed holding period is to take the reciprocal of the fund's turnover rate times 12. For example, if the turnover rate were 60% the fixed holding period would be computed as: $(1/.60) \times 12$ months $= 20$ months. Examining the results based on a range of fixed holding periods might be constructive in assessing how sensitive the results of this analysis are to this assumption.

Chapter 7

1. The values for the three basic skills sum up to the fund's relative return.

2. Unlike the measures of basic skills, which are absolute, the analysis of sector skills is relative. Consequently, they do not add up to, or average to, the total buy skill. What's important is that the higher the value, the more skilled the buys are in a sector, while the lower or more negative the value, the less skilled.

3. Analyst ranks are the result of deep company investigations, market research, competitive analyses, and discounted cash-flow projections. Analyst ranks are sometimes in the form of numeric values (e.g., 1 = underpriced stock or strong alpha potential and 10 = overpriced and weak alpha potential). Alternatively, analyst recommendations may be provided as statements (e.g., strong buy, buy, hold, sell, strong sell).

Chapter 8

1. Attributes are the financial characteristics of a stock and its underlying company. Attributes can include standard fundamental factors, quantitative factors, results or alpha scores from a quantitative model, and research analyst rankings. The examples presented use sector-relative attribute values, which facilitates the comparison of stocks across sectors.

2. *Investable universe* refers to the stocks the fund actually considers for ownership. Often the fund's benchmark constituents are its investable universe. Some funds may exclude certain benchmark stocks or include nonbenchmark stocks within their investable universe.

3. The date of the initial buy is used in that it best represents the date when the decision to buy was made and therefore is representative of the information available to the research analyst or manager.

4. Hill climbing is a simple optimization algorithm used in artificial intelligence to find the best possible solution for a given problem. It belongs to the family of local search algorithms and is often used in optimization problems where the goal is to find the best solution from a set of possible solutions. "Introduction to Hill Climbing," GeeksforGeeks, accessed May 23, 2024, https://www.geeksforgeeks.org.

Chapter 9

1. Naturally, there are other considerations to be taken into account regarding which position to sell, such as risk exposures, tracking error, and the financial characteristics of stocks on the short list of potential new buys.

2. This involves the daily calculation of each position age, determining the fund's median position age, comparing each position's age to the fund's median age, and

then sorting all positions as younger (i.e., less than the median) or older (i.e., greater than the median). See chapter 5 for more details regarding the computation of position age.

3. An *unrealized gain* refers to a position that from the time of its initial purchase through the earlier of its sell date or the date of an analysis outperformed its sector return. An *unrealized loss* refers to a position that from the time of its initial purchase through the earlier of its sell date or the date of an analysis underperformed its sector return.

4. This example assumes that the position is completely sold. When adjusting for a trim, a similar process is used. The distinction is that the amount of the position repurchased is sold not when the position achieves the fund's median age but on the date the position is actually liquidated in the fund.

5. The advanced sell date could be later if, on the date when the older winner's age equals the fund's median age, the position is not then a winner. The sell would be delayed until the first day thereafter that the position has an unrealized gain.

6. The results for the individual sell timing skills do not add up to the fund's basic sell skill. This is due to the cross-effects of delaying some actions while advancing others. Thus, a range of the fund's basic sell skill is presented. In practice, the fund's actual basic sell skill is available for reference.

Chapter 10

1. Interim sizing decisions (adds and trims) have been found to be unproductive within the majority of approximately 2,000 professionally managed funds that have been analyzed by Inalytics Ltd., Alpha Theory LLC, and Cabot Investment Technology Inc., a subsidiary of FactSet Research Systems Inc.

2. The inflows, outflows, funding purchases, and reabsorbing sales proceeds can be managed through pro rata adds and trims. These pro rata trades maintain position weights and therefore are not actions. The likely exception is risk management trades, which are likely to require other than pro rata activity.

3. Each of the four counterfactuals created can be subject to interaction effects with or from another counterfactual. For example, a position ABC might have received an add early on and then been trimmed not long after. The impact of the add to position ABC would be computed as part of one counterfactual. The impact of the trim would be computed in another. The combined or net effect cannot be ascertained simply by adding the results of two or more counterfactuals. The benefit presented is suggestive of what may be the combined effects from all four skills.

4. This estimate is based on the analysis of over $4 trillion of professionally managed equities, involving hundreds of funds, conducted by Cabot Investment Technology Inc., a subsidiary of FactSet Research Systems Inc.

5. The image presented in figure 10.6 is known as a holdings report or stock page. It details when an active position is initially established (i.e., fund weight exceeds benchmark weight), each subsequent add and trim (i.e., actions based on weight changes), and the eventual sell (i.e., fund weight dips below benchmark weight).

6. Michael A. Ervolini and Andrew R. Tuttle, "When Buying Low and Selling High Destroy Alpha: Visualizing the Interplay Amongst Judgment, Process, and the Disposition Effect," August 2025. An abstract is available at www.skillversusluck.com.

Chapter 11

1. Daniel Kahneman and Amos Tversky, "Prospect Theory: An Analysis of Decision Under Risk," *Econometrica* 47 (March 1979): 263–292. Also see Richard H. Thaler and Eric J. Johnson, "Gambling with the House Money and Trying to Break Even: The Effects of Prior Outcomes on Risky Choice," *Management Science* 36 (June 1990), https://doi.org/10.1287/mnsc.36.6.643.

2. Huixin Tan, Qin Duan, Yihan Liu, Xinyu Qiao, and Siyang Luo, "Does Losing Money Truly Hurt? The Shared Neural Bases of Monetary Loss and Pain," *Human Brain Mapping* 43 (2022): 3153–3163.

3. David Tuckett and Richard Taffler, "Fund Management: An Emotional Finance Perspective," CFA Institute Research Foundation, 2012.

4. The assessment of factor levels is based on sector-relative comparisons as of the day the position meets the threshold level. A more detailed description of how sector-relative factor levels are computed is provided in chapter 9.

Chapter 12

1. The discussion presented in this chapter concerns the buildup of new buys. Some funds buy stocks that, on average, experience significant price increases soon after purchase (i.e., front-loaded returns). Other funds more often buy stocks that linger for weeks and months before showing signs of price movement (i.e., back-loaded returns). This topic is discussed further in chapter 4.

2. A position's contribution to fund return is computed as its fund weight times its return, over the period being analyzed. A position with a high return combined with a small fund weight will generate less contribution than the same stock with a higher fund weight.

3. Ultimately, a fund's returns are the sum of its buying, sizing, and selling skills. In the present discussion, the selling skill is assumed to be neutral at worst or possibly a positive skill.

4. A fund's full weight refers to the typical full active weight given to positions plus the positions benchmark weight. The size of the active portion can vary over time as the fund's total active weight and number of positions change. A further description of active weight and its formulation is found in chapter 5.

Chapter 13

1. The charts and graphs used in this case study are based on an actual actively managed equity fund. Some of the fund descriptive information is obfuscated to preserve the anonymity of the fund. The allocation team narratives are the product of literary license.

2. The sum of the three basic skills (buying, selling, and sizing) equals the fund's relative return.

3. Analyses of over $4 trillion equity assets involving hundreds of funds conducted by Cabot Investment Technology Inc. and FactSet Research Systems Inc. show that less than 15% of funds reflect positive values across buying, selling, and sizing skills. While not a proper statistical sample of the entire universe of equity funds, the group of funds analyzed is substantial and its results are informative.

4. Description of how each of the analytics presented are computed can be found in the proceeding chapters. The exception is the analytic referred to as Add Up. This analytic is based on the difference of the actual fund and three distinct counterfactual portfolios. Having reviewed the previous chapters, the reader will be able to conceptually appreciate how this analytic is computed.

5. Ramp-up analysis examines whether a fund's winners are being brought up to their full weight in a timely fashion. The analysis is similar to others discussed in detail in this book, involving computing the difference between the results of the actual fund and one or more counterfactual portfolios. The accelerated time periods shown (immediate, two months, four months) indicate when the accelerated buildup commences. In each instance, the time to reach full position weight is governed by the observed tolerance of the fund to incur market impact. In other words, when building up positions immediately, the likely time to complete this ramping up invariably takes many days or weeks.

6. Detailed descriptions of how each of the four sell timing results are computed are presented in chapter 10.

Chapter 14

1. Akepanidtaworn, Di Mascio, Imas, and Schmidt, "Selling Fast and Buying Slow."

2. I am the founder and former CEO of Cabot Investment Technology Inc. After its purchase by FactSet, I worked with the company from July 2021 until February

2024. Since that time I have had no financial relationship with FactSet. FactSet was tremendously gracious in allowing me the use of scores of graphs, plots, and visualizations used in this book.

3. See chapter 5 for a description of how actions are computed and used to quantify skills.

4. See chapter 6 for a description of how counterfactual portfolios are constructed and used to compute the buy, sell, and sizing skills.

5. For more details on the FactSet-Cabot skill analytics, see Ervolini, *Managing Equity Portfolios*.

6. Information concerning the Touring Technology Associates' beta test was obtained from their LinkedIn page on November 21, 2024.

Publisher contact:
The MIT Press
Massachusetts Institute of Technology
77 Massachusetts Avenue, Cambridge, MA 02139
mitpress.mit.edu

EU Authorised Representative:
Easy Access System Europe, Mustamäe tee 50,
10621 Tallinn, Estonia
gpsr.requests@easproject.com

Printed by Integrated Books International,
United States of America